THE YOUNG HORSE:
Breaking and Training

THE YOUNG HORSE:
Breaking and Training

Jennie Loriston-Clarke

Photographs by Bob Langrish

Trafalgar Square Publishing

First published in the United States of America in 1995 by
Trafalgar Square Publishing, North Pomfret, Vermont 05053
First published in paperback 1999
Printed in Italy by New Interlitho SpA

ISBN 1–57076–130–2
Library of Congress Catalog Card Number: 98–85574

Contents

Dance in the Dark and Zebedee in the Bourne river

Introduction

In this book I have tried to give an insight into the way we progress with a young and inexperienced horse, how we teach him to be a willing and obedient partner and educate him until he is ready to enter the competitive field in any discipline. You may ask why it is important to balance and collect a horse when it is quite possible just to sit on his back and change from one pace to another with no technique at all. This is fine if all you want to do is to hack around the woods and fields; but when you have ridden a properly balanced and well-trained horse the difference is as great as that between driving a Mini and a Rolls-Royce: the one is jerky and bumpy, the other smooth, powerful and light to the touch.

Every young horse will become wilful and disobedient if he is not educated, even to the point of becoming a danger to himself and other people if not kept properly under control. He will also be on his forehand; *but* if you teach him to carry himself so that he is able to balance himself correctly and carry the rider, then he will lighten the forehand and will inevitably be much more responsive to the rider's aids. There is no doubt that medals are won by the combinations of horse and rider that are the best trained and the most responsive to each other, and it is this feeling of partnership which is so wonderful and so important: the horse must completely trust his rider, and the rider must also have the ability to go with his horse and to trust him in whatever he is asking him to do. It is important that training is progressive, that when a new task is learned it is followed by a period of practice to try and perfect what you have learned. This process continues throughout a horse's training. Sometimes you may find you have overdone a particular part of the training programme, and then it is important to appreciate that you may have to regress a few steps in order to build up your confidence in each other again.

A horse is not a machine: they all have their differences and no horse can ever be made like another, nor must you force or try to curb his natural character; however, a horse must not be allowed to get his own way, either, nor to behave in a way which could become a potentially dangerous habit. The horse is a very strong and powerful animal, and out of control he can be violent and intimidating; incorrectly handled, many might show these traits – and yet with the correct touch these same horses can settle down and become docile and amenable. It is impossible to match strength with strength; a horse weighs approximately half a ton, so technique and understanding are very important: your sensitivity and

Dance in the Dark looking at his first step-down fence

your ability to assess the horse's attitude and comprehension are paramount.

When a horse is educated to be ridden under saddle, he must be taught right from the start to carry himself so that he can carry the weight of the rider with ease and balance, and use his muscles and joints with greater elasticity so that he is a more comfortable and balanced ride. He is then able to be really responsive: his hind legs and body are more able to manoeuvre both his own weight and that of his rider, and he is in a better position and one hopes frame of mind to listen and react to the wishes of his rider in a willing and obedient manner.

In this book we describe the

progressive stages of training which we follow, and we hope it will help all those intending to school their horses to the point where they have the experience and physical ability to cope with the early competitions of dressage, showjumping and cross-country – and beyond! The horse which is supple, obedient and willing will always come ahead of a horse that is constantly fighting the aids of the rider, as this inharmonious approach will inevitably cause him to be stiff in his back and will prevent him from being able to use his limbs correctly and with looseness, resulting in lack of rhythm in his paces, and in stiffness and tension which will cause faults when jumping.

Chapter 1

Selecting the Competition Horse

What makes you think you have a showjumper, an event horse or a dressage horse? Often there is not much difference when you assess conformation. The horse's natural paces are more important for dressage, as are temperament and willingness. Where the parentage of successful, proven performers is known, it is shown time and again that such horses do produce winners, or certainly horses more likely, with correct training, to excel in the disciplines for which they are bred. It has also been shown that a horse bred to showjump will often make a good dressage horse, provided his paces are correct; and this is true the other way about, too.

The event horse is usually pure thoroughbred, or three-quarter thoroughbred where the out-cross is either Irish Draught, a Continental warmblood or native pony. Thoroughbred blood is needed for speed, stamina and particularly courage, since without courage the eventer is useless; some bloodlines are keenly sought after because these qualities of courage and trust are particularly prevalent in the offspring. Obviously a great deal depends on the training and riding of these horses, but there is little point in using horses which are known to be bad performers; horses that have shown exceptional courage in competition and have won,

tough, genuine horses – these are the ones to breed from, and this is as true for mares as it is for stallions. A horse which has hunted, evented or showjumped for several seasons and stayed sound is more likely to produce good, sound, workmanlike offspring than a second-rate, brokendown animal that would never start.

Natural ability can often be observed in the very young horse, too, sometimes even as young as a foal. A foal that will happily jump clumps of nettles, fallen branches and ditches with natural ease and technique is perhaps a jumping prospect; and those that lead the herd at weaning time are perhaps most likely to be bold and forward-going across country. Foals with natural carriage and loose, athletic movement showing swing and elasticity in all their paces are usually dressage prospects – Catherston Dazzler and Catherston Dutch Bid, for example. The dressage horse must have presence, and that inimitable star quality; he must also have considerable courage and be forward-thinking, level-headed and willing to please.

A horse with natural jumping talent is generally fairly bold and has a good lift to the shoulders. When jumping he must be careful in his approach, and show a good lift to the knees with flexion of the forelegs; a horse that leaves his knees dangling when jumping is disliked, and is not usually a safe ride. The good jumper should look fluent and effortless in action, allowing his hind legs to flow out behind him. Jumpers come in all sorts and sizes, from thoroughbreds to warmbloods; many are half- or three-quarter bred, a thoroughbred stallion crossed with an Irish or warmblood mare. The modern showjumper must have scope and be very athletic; it needs quality and a good stride to be able to cope with the long distances in combination fences as well as the agility to shorten the stride and lift the shoulders and knees correctly in order to jump big fences after quick turns in a jump off.

For competition work, correct conformation and action will give the horse a better chance of staying sound throughout training and in his competitive career, although nowadays the modern trend of longer seasons has resulted in fewer horses working into their late teens than there used to be, however good their make and shape. Twenty years ago all competition horses would have at least three months' rest over the winter months as the showing and jumping seasons would finish at the end of the summer, but now there are big competitions for showjumpers and show and dressage horses all the year round. It is therefore a great temptation to over-expose a good horse, and the stress and strain of travel and competition undoubtedly take their toll on its legs and general physique.

Dutch Courage: a proud horse with lots of presence and a bold outlook. He has very strong quarters with hocks well let down, his head is set well, and he has a naturally high head carriage. He is a little long in the back, but this never affected his amazing suppleness and athletic ability

Catherston Humbug, a lovely type of young dressage horse, with a good shoulder and neck coming nicely from the wither. He shows presence and quality, and has a good short and strong back, making a correct outline

Everest Milton, the world's greatest showjumper. This horse has tremendous quality and a noble outlook, and correct conformation; it is no surprise that he has been so successful

Everest Monsanta: a wonderful horse, whose bold heart and willingness to please have made him more successful than his conformation might otherwise indicate. He has a great depth of girth, is 'butty' and quite short-legged, which one might expect would limit his scope, but he has certainly proved to have everything one could ask for in a genuine showjumper

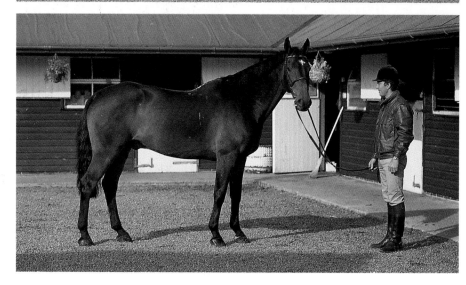

The eventer Three Royals, a very quality thoroughbred mare with a good neck well set on to a lovely shoulder, and a good foreleg. She has a short back with strong loin muscles, and well proportioned quarters. She has quite a long hind leg, and the hocks are set a little high. This horse is correctly turned out for the showjumping phase in horse trials

Xenocles, a lovely thoroughbred stallion with a short, strong back, good quarters and a good hind leg with his hocks well under the body. The foreleg is a little upright in the pastern, and slightly back at the knee. He proved himself as an Advanced eventer, and also bred bold performers

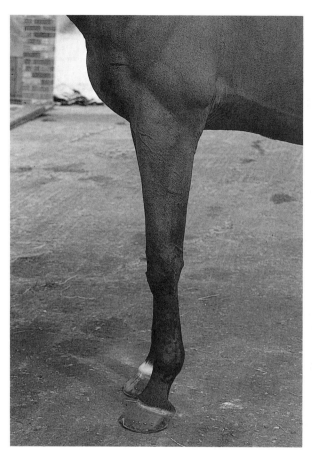

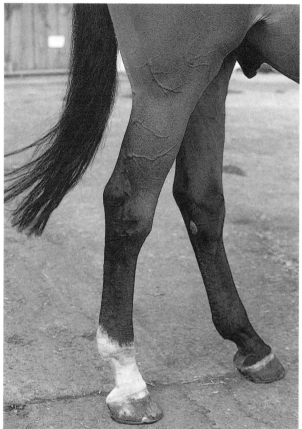

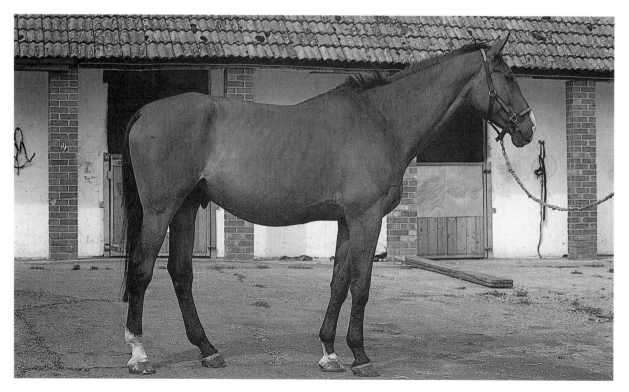

(Far left) Short, upright pasterns

(Left) Straight hocks

(Below left) A low-set neck

(Left) A bowed tendon

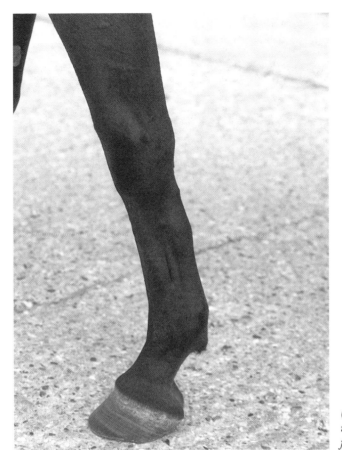

(Below) A short hind leg with sickle hocks set away from the body

CONFORMATION FOR SOUNDNESS

The head should be neat and well set on to the neck so there is room for the horse to flex – the bottom jaw should not be too deep, and the teeth should be correctly aligned. The eye should be large, generous and kind, the ears not too small and pricked forwards; ears will always give you an indication of temperament, and a horse which habitually puts his ears back could be ungenerous and mean. The ears and the eyes tell you most about a horse's character: I have always found that a horse which looks you in the eye and comes to talk to you

for who *you* are, and not for a titbit, is the one who works for you best.

The neck should be reasonably long and have good muscle on the upper crest line, depending on the horse's age and the work it has done. Always look at the underline of the neck, and particularly the distance from the shoulder to the lower jaw – the length should fit the overall size of the horse, and the muscle in the lower half of the neck should never be greater than in the upper half; if it is, this is probably a horse that doesn't carry himself well.

The neck topline should come out of the shoulder as high as possible, and from the withers to the poll should describe an uphill rounded shape, the whole neck

Polly Flinders: this heavy cob pony hardly looks like a showjumper, but when motivated and thinking forwards jumped five clear rounds in one day, could jump up to 1.5m (5 feet) from a trot, and won the Richmond Jumping Championships as a rank outsider!

finally attaching to the top of the head in a svelte and elegant way. Horses with too big a lower jaw often find it more difficult to flex their head and neck. The shoulder should be sloping with the withers clearly defined, and the muscles on the shoulder should be well developed. The chest should be reasonably wide, and the foreleg set on at the elbow with adequate freedom for loose movement.

The forelegs should be straight, and the knee well let down with short cannon bones. The horse should not be 'back at the knee' – this throws too much strain on the tendons – and the weight should come down the foreleg straight, running to the middle of the hoof. The fetlock joint should be at the correct angle, and the pastern should be springy but not too long.

The hoof should be strong, and with good horn, the correct shape and in balance with the limb. The heels should be firm and well defined, with the toes correctly in balance with the heels.

The back should be of medium length with well-developed back muscles and strong over the loin. The depth of girth should fit the length of leg and look in proportion. A heavy-topped horse will put more strain on its legs. The quarters should match the trunk of the horse, and the croup should be strong.

The hind leg should have good angles down its entire length, from hip to stifle, stifle to hock, hock to fetlock, and fetlock to hoof; it should stand under the horse, and not away from it. When standing behind the horse the hind leg should be seen to be taking the weight from the pelvis through the hock to the hoof in a straight line; there should be no deviation through the hock either inwards or outwards to the hoof.

MOVEMENT

The Dressage Horse

For dressage, the horse must have a good clear walk with the hind foot able to overstep the print of the fore foot by a clear margin, preferably 15 – 20cm at least when asked to walk on. There must be a clear four-time beat and no tendency for the horse to move with a lateral beat or pace. The walk is the most difficult pace to improve so needs to be studied carefully. When excited, a horse will generally tense up and make the walk look irregular; with correct training and education these more excitable horses can be improved.

The trot must be powerful with a clear two-time beat, and with a natural cadence and rhythm; the horse should also show a good overtrack in working trot and use the knees and hocks freely. Stiff, staccato movers may look impressive but they often find it difficult to extend. The looseness and elasticity of the steps is more important for the future than paces which may look impressive to start with, but are stiff; if there is no suppleness, flexibility or power from within the joints, the horse will find the more demanding dressage movements very hard indeed.

The canter should have a clear three-time beat, and be balanced and united; the hocks should come well under the body and be able to carry the weight of the horse in easy balance. There should be a good moment of suspension when all four feet are off the ground before the next step. The pace should be light and cadenced and have regular strides.

The Eventer

The walk should demonstrate the same qualities as for the dressage

Dutch Courage in piaffe in front of Goodwood House, aged 15 years. Most of the Catherston horses have Dutch Courage in their pedigree

horse, but as event horses are so often thoroughbreds they generally have a very big overtrack, a good swing and a long, ground-covering stride. Their trot, however, is often not quite as pronounced in the moment of suspension since they move closer to the ground; nevertheless they should show freedom and rhythm in the trot and be able to lengthen the strides, and as in all paces, should travel with swing and elasticity. The trot should be a ground-covering, effortless pace so that the horse takes as little out of himself as possible in the roads and tracks section of the endurance phase.

The canter must be balanced and loose, and the horse must be able to lengthen and shorten the steps easily in order to achieve the collection and agility required to jump the bounces and combination fences typical of today's cross-country courses. The strides must be fluid and ground-covering; a short-striding horse uses up too much energy in the endurance phase, and usually lacks scope over the larger spreads.

The gallop is an important pace in three-day eventing: many points can be lost on the steeplechase if a horse cannot gallop with the good rhythm and cadence necessary to achieve the speed required. A horse that cannot relax into his gallop, but goes along in a short-striding, unrhythmical and tense manner will find this phase difficult; he will expend a great deal of energy and become far more stressed. A horse that pulls or is sluggish will also waste both your energy and his. It is up to you to assess whether you will be able to improve this pace in a horse with schooling and practice.

The Showjumper

The walk is not so important, although a good free walk does show

that the horse has adequate freedom in his shoulders and back. The trot should be active, especially the hind legs which should come well under the body; the horse should have good free action in the forelegs, and be loose and athletic with a springing back.

The canter should be balanced and springy, with the hind legs coming well under the body. The horse must be able to lengthen and shorten the strides and show a good natural rhythm.

TEMPERAMENT

Temperament is an important factor in all disciplines, and the horse must genuinely want to work and be keen to please the rider. Most young horses are bound to have a few lapses when they try to get their own way, but with correct training they can usually be directed into pleasing you willingly. Different riders prefer different temperaments, and what one person dislikes another will like, sometimes almost intuitively – a classic example of this sort of telepathic empathy occurred when I went out to Holland to look for a good young horse. I visited one farm and was shown a mare which did nothing for me at all, but on my way back to the car I saw another head poking over a high door – I was immediately attracted, and asked the farmer's wife if I could see that horse. She said I couldn't, explaining that the horse was a stallion and was intended to be a showjumper, and would probably soon be gelded.

After seeing many other horses in Holland we returned to this farm, as I had a feeling that this horse behind the high door was something special. The farmer had 'flu, but after much persuasion he was dragged from his bed as anything

could be for sale! Sure enough, this horse had that look in his ears and eyes that just clicked with me; he had courage, presence and charisma and he looked me in the eye when I talked to him. The chemistry clicked and we made a deal with the farmer and his wife.

This horse was Dutch Courage, who taught me so much and did so much not only for me, but for dressage and for the breeding of competition horses in this country.

Manageability is also important and inevitably linked to temperament: a horse that is basically quiet in the stable and able to relax is much less likely to

become stressed, whereas a very sharp, flighty horse can be difficult to settle, and it often takes a long time to persuade him to concentrate on his work; he will take a lot more out of himself if he frets when travelling, and will take longer to settle in a new environment or a strange stable – along with the fact that he will probably need more working in before the competition itself.

I have also had horses that have appeared to be quite unmanageable when handled from the ground, but have settled down as soon as they have been given something positive to do, such as trotting over poles on the ground or a session of serious flatwork to occupy their minds. Often these are very good horses which like work and are only difficult when they are bored. Dutch Courage was like this and so are some of his offspring, always anxious to keep you mentally active and needing to be kept busy with learning things new in order to occupy their minds; and in fact this can give you the edge above quieter horses, since when you require maximum effort they are always ready to respond. For top-class competition you do need a horse which is quick and responsive, yet able to relax and settle to his environment easily; and a horse which relates to his rider and has a quick response to the aids is an asset in any discipline. The event horse has to have complete trust and the ability to think quickly if he is to perform the amazing feats of jumping demanded in the cross-country course, when so often he cannot even see where he is landing. Trust in the rider is of paramount importance in this discipline, although it takes a great deal of time and patience in training to achieve.

This horse is approaching a cross-country fence. Note the attention of both horse and rider: the horse is completely settled in his mind in that he is not pulling or fighting the rider in any way. He is therefore ready to comply with the rider's wishes, keeping a rhythm up to the fence. This picture shows confidence and trust

Early Relationships

The good trainer will have studied the horse's natural reactions to various situations, and will always have in mind that the horse is a herd animal which originally lived wild; its senses of hearing, sight, smell, taste and touch are therefore acutely developed. In order to train an animal you must develop a sympathetic understanding as to why it reacts to certain situations in the way it does: it doesn't necessarily think the way we do, and besides, every horse has a different personality – you must learn to study each as an individual and try to analyse its reactions to different situations. Learn to watch a horse's ears – perhaps he has heard something which you haven't. A hunter will hear hounds long before you will, and if you are aware of this when lost you may well find your way back to join the field.

The horse's sight has been a point for discussion for many years, particularly as to whether a horse sees colours in the same way that we do. Why do some coloured poles cause some horses more spooks than others? The eye of the horse will generally reflect his state of mind, revealing whether he is nervous and frightened, relaxed and calm, or wicked and naughty. The eyes and the ears usually move together and indicate exactly how he feels.

His senses of smell and taste are extremely sensitive: a dead animal or a natural aversion to pigs may provoke a quite violent reaction; a stallion will immediately sense an in-season mare. The horse is often a very fussy feeder, and can easily be put off if he smells or tastes anything new in his food or water. Some horses are highly sensitive to touch, particularly if highly strung and in a strange situation. Often this sort will hardly tolerate a grooming brush because they are so thin-skinned; this could become a neurotic problem, so use a cactus cloth or a stable rubber and a very soft brush firmly and quietly. You must be aware that when a horse is nervous about being touched it is his instinctive reaction to predatorial attack: it is therefore vital to use a very relaxed and quiet arm. The horse's natural instinct is to escape danger through flight, but it will attack if cornered by kicking, biting or rearing and striking out with the forelegs; if jumped on by a predator its instinct is to buck and bite to dislodge it, as well as to flee. It is important not to react with anger if a horse appears spooky or difficult.

Some horses seem to have a natural sixth sense of danger: this will guide them to avoiding bogs, unsafe bridges and dangerous ramps on lorries; sometimes it will take the form of a homing instinct, and they will unerringly bring you home when you are not sure of the way.

Teaching a youngster to let you pick up his feet when asked: first stroke each leg from the elbow to the foot

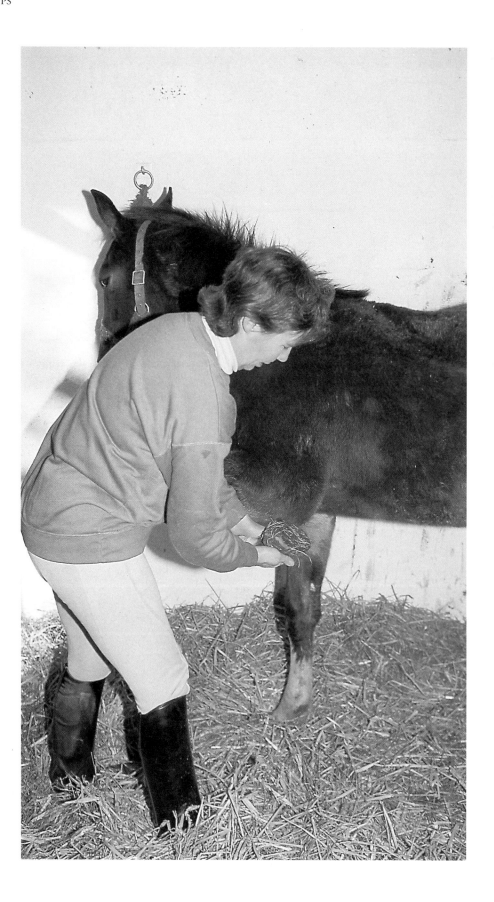

Do the same behind: stroke the leg from the hock to the foot

Gradually the foal must learn to lead – he must walk forwards in response to light pressure on the lead-rein

HANDLING THE FOAL

It is very important to handle a foal in the first few weeks of its life, and this contact is something it never forgets. We like to handle a foal all over, feeling its ears, opening its mouth, picking up its feet and washing its tail. We will lead it every day for the first month, starting with a cloth round its neck and progressing to a foal-slip after a week. Use the words of command, 'walk on' and 'woah', as this will help you both in later life.

We proceed as follows: put the cloth or towel round the foal's neck and hold it in the left hand; put the right hand behind the foal's quarters, encouraging it to move forwards and follow its mother. This is a good way to start, but after a few days you should progress to leading with a foal-slip or headcollar. Foals are very sensitive about their muzzle,

Leading a young foal with a cloth round his neck held in the left hand, and with the right hand round his quarters to encourage him forwards

Teaching a foal to lead: here the mare is being led from the off side, with the foal leading well and walking confidently on the near side. Try to remember to remove your spurs when working with horses on the ground!

and special care must be taken when putting on the foal-slip. To do this, position the mare in the corner of the stable – put a headcollar and a bridle on her if you intend to lead her out, unless you know her well and can control her easily. With the mare in the corner you can attempt to catch the foal: let it get close to its mother and then, using mum as a buffer, approach it from the side; quickly and quietly get one arm round its neck and one round the quarters, and turn it so that its quarters are towards the wall and its mother – then if it runs back when you put the foal-slip on it won't hurt itself.

Now, standing on the near side and holding the foal between you and the wall with mother on the off side, open the foal-slip up below its chin with your hands either side of its neck, and gently put the noseband over its nose, taking care not to touch its quite long whiskers; if it is very head-shy then it is sometimes easier to put your left hand on the bridge of the nose while you slip the noseband on with

the right hand. Quiet insistence will usually win the day, and then you can adjust the slip so that it is fitting correctly. Put a lead-rein on, and lead in a similar way as with the cloth, keeping your hand behind the quarters as before with only a very light feel on the head-slip. I find moving the mare around the stable and getting the foal to follow with a light feel on the rein and your right hand behind the quarters gets it used to the feel of the foal-slip before you progress to moving in a straight line outside.

In these early days, some studs just pull the rope through the foal-slip and hold it double so you can let go if you get into trouble without the fear of the foal getting tangled up in a dangling rope; but take care that this does not become a habit, with the foal learning to pull away in order to get away from you. If you keep the foal close to its dam on her near side this will help in keeping it straight, and provided you can maintain this position things should go well; but sometimes foals pull back, and a few

Teaching a foal to stand: position the foal to stand correctly, with the mare nearby to give it confidence, and then move away a little to let the foal stand almost on its own

Leading mare and foal together: lead the foal with the left hand, and put the right hand behind its quarters to keep it moving forwards after the mare

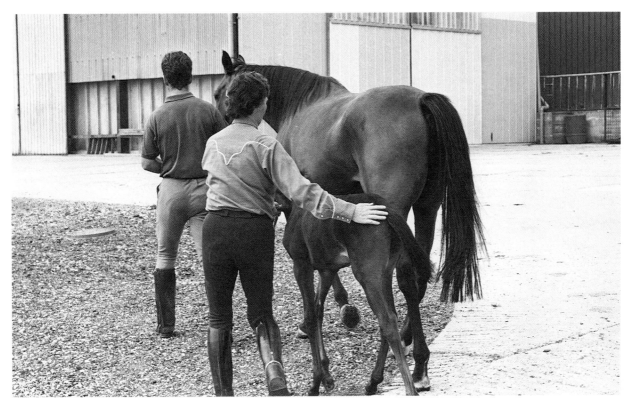

will try and throw themselves right over backwards. Obviously this is a dangerous circumstance and can damage the foal badly, so every effort should be made to keep it alongside the handler – always keep the right hand there to push the foal forwards if necessary. As the foal gets used to being led you can gradually dispense with the right hand, and lead the foal with the rein in the normal manner. Some foals are very independent and are quite happy to lead a little way from their dams. We find it quite helpful to show our mares and foals a few times; the foal is then well handled, and becomes thoroughly accustomed to travelling, and loading into and out of the lorry, and to all the sights and sounds of a horse show.

Some people loose jump their foals; I never do this, as any knock on a joint could inflict an injury which might cause unsoundness when the animal is mature. The joints are so soft at this age, and I feel that there is plenty of time for it to show itself when you come to break and school it – although I

often note a foal's natural style and enthusiasm when he jumps a clump of nettles or a dip in the ground. Catherston Zulu, for example, showed particular jumping ability as a foal.

Take care of the foal's feet; get your farrier to study him from both the front and the side to make sure the balance of his feet is correct. Make a point of noticing the angle of the foot/pastern/fetlock, as any abnormality will indicate that he is growing too fast; remember that more trouble is caused by overfeeding than underfeeding a foal. He should be wormed every month.

HANDLING OLDER HORSES

A horse which has not been handled as a foal or yearling will almost certainly be fairly wild and nervous, and you will have to take time to accustom him to the human touch. As we have observed already, a horse is a timid animal and will run away if frightened; however, he is also by nature inquisitive, and you can use this to your advantage. I like to let a new horse settle in a large stable, giving him plenty of time to get used to seeing me feed and water him. (Do not feed many concentrates: this is unnecessary if he is not going to have a lot of exercise.) Take your time when going into the stable; talk to him, maybe feed him a little sweet-smelling hay by hand. It helps if he wears a loose-fitting headcollar with a short rope attached, about 30cm (12in) long; if you can quietly get hold of it each time you are talking to the horse or feeding him, he will quite quickly show less fright when you go to touch him. However, to put a headcollar on a wild horse can take a bit of time!

MARES AND FOALS AT GRASS
If you are going to turn your mare and foal out with headcollars on, it is much safer to use leather ones; if they get caught on anything leather will break, but nylon ones are often too strong and can throttle a foal. Take special notice that there is enough room round the noseband for mare and foal to eat properly; a foal's head grows very fast so it is essential to remember to let it out every week or more. I have often been sent mares and foals rubbed raw under their headcollars, and this is pure cruelty and neglect – it is no excuse for people to say they 'couldn't catch him', and if every time you touch the headcollar it hurts him, it is hardly surprising if he *does* become head-shy. We never leave a headcollar on either mare or foal when they are turned out in the field, unless there is a specific reason for doing so.

First of all he may not let you even touch him, and may persistently turn his backside towards you. In this case I would chase him away from me with a lunge rein, although you must realise that he might kick at you so make sure you are out of reach; however, you must also not step away from him, or he will feel that by kicking he has the upper hand. If he is a real kicker then a lunge whip will give you more safety and more distance. Point the whip towards his flank or hind leg and if he kicks at it give him a smart flick until he runs forward from it; hopefully he will then turn and snort at you as he takes stock of this situation. You may have to flick the whip at him a few times until he will stay and look at you. Then, talking very quietly, gently approach him on the near side: be aware that he could turn away from you at any time, so keep looking at his ears and eyes – but be very calm and relaxed yourself. Move forwards a little, then retreat a bit, then move forwards again until he begins to relax a little himself. As you get nearer, let him first sniff your hand and then gradually stroke his shoulder; horses like to be scratched a bit on the shoulder and around the withers. If you can do this, then you will get him to relax quickly as this is the usual way for horses to groom each other, and he will come to accept you; if he does not, rub him gently on the shoulder and move away again.

Once you have done this a few times he will be more prepared to accept you, so go in this time with an adjustable headcollar, undone at the noseband as well as the headpiece, and with a cotton rope to place round his neck first. Approach him and touch him with the rope coiled up in your hand, and quietly let the end fall over the neck as far up his crest at he will allow. Talk to him all the time and gently take hold of both ends so that you now have a little control over him. Soothe him again, and gradually pass the headcollar headpiece round his neck and do it up – though it may take several attempts! Then holding on to him with the right hand on the headcollar, stroke his cheek with the left hand, gradually moving up to the bridge of his nose. As he gets used to this feeling you can pass the nosepiece of the headcollar up to your left hand, the right hand passing it up from behind his chin. This may take you a few minutes, gently playing around with him all the while, but it will be time well spent.

Make sure the headcollar is correctly fitted, and then attach a short rope of approximately 30cm (12in) which you could leave on him provided the stable is safe. When you have hold of him stroke him gently on the shoulder and neck, put a longer lead rope on him and then gradually rub him all over with your hand; scratch him at the base of the neck just in front of the withers, and also around the shoulder area where he might appreciate a rub. If he enjoys it, he will relax; if he looks apprehensive then stop, and handle him where he feels happy. Take your time, and keep an eye on his eyes and ears to see how he is reacting. Never do more than he is happy to let you do; be very patient, and very quiet and relaxed in yourself; if *you* are tense, no amount of handling will help as he will feel the tension in you and be worried, and will therefore not trust you.

When you have established a degree of trust with your horse, you must teach him to lead and to listen to you, to move out of your space and to turn to left and right, to step

Teaching a horse to tie up

Initially the horse appears tense; the lunge rein is threaded through the wall ring and back to the handler, who must keep a relatively light but constant pressure on the rein whatever the horse does, until he settles and comes back to the wall: then he must straightaway be rewarded by a lightening of the contact, and the handler can come forwards to pat him and reassure him

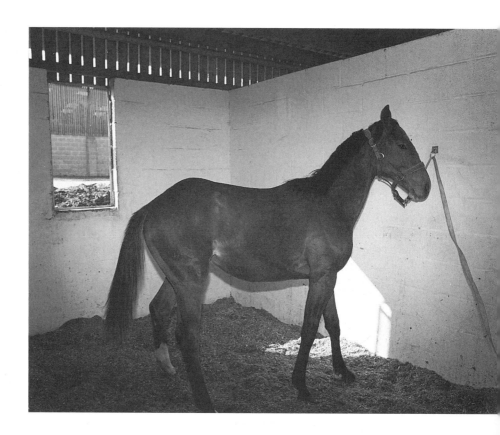

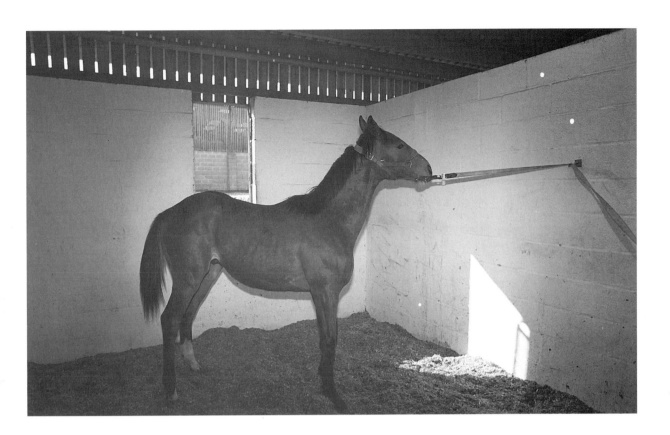

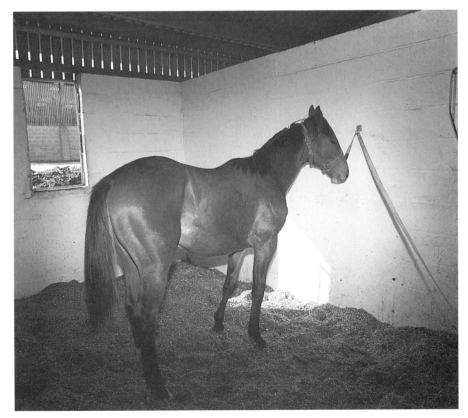

A useful way of leading a young horse which is a bit strong: the chain threads through the near-side ring, twists over and behind the material of the noseband and clips on to the off-side ring. Some horses lunge more happily in this headcollar and chain arrangement than they do in a cavesson; it also teaches them not to lean on the handler. It is vital that the hand contact is sympathetic – only use a firm pull when you need to. A horse should never be tied up by this headcollar and chain arrangement

back and to come forwards. To do this, put a long lead-rope on to the headcollar or cavesson and take a schooling whip so that you can touch him with it should he not walk up beside you. Take him to an enclosed area or barn and lead him about: this is your first opportunity to teach him the commands of 'walk on' and 'woah'. Hold the rein at least 30cm (12in) from the cavesson or headcollar with your right hand, with the end of the rein and whip in your left hand. Say 'walk on' and as you do so, move slightly yourself and at the same time; if he doesn't move, touch him with the whip behind you – the end of the schooling whip should touch the horse on the left flank and encourage him to move forwards. As he does so, reward him with your voice. First move on a left-handed circle so that the horse learns to move with you and to go forwards. Teach him to walk on, and to stop. Be consistent with your voice commands.

When he is concentrating and obedient to your commands, then you must teach him to turn to the right. For this he must let you move round him; this is where you must teach him to 'steady' – a little light pressure on the rein and voice steadies the walk. Look him in the eye and make him turn slowly to the right, collecting his weight more on to his hind legs as he makes the turn. Some people raise the left hand when doing this, but I prefer not to as I have seen many horses made head-shy in this way – then they turn their heads away from you and push at you with their shoulders, and this is a dangerous habit. When the horse has remained steady and let you walk round him, then walk on again; repeat the exercise several times. When this is achieved, try a few steps of trot in

hand, with the correct commands: this is the first stage of showing him off and teaching him the commands.

He must learn to stand, and to back up when asked. Teach him this as follows: once he has halted with your saying 'woah' and with him standing beside you, then move yourself round so you are standing in front of him and insist that he stays where he is. I like to do this because a horse has to learn that he must not walk over you, also that he should retreat when looked in the eye. Stroking his forehead will be appreciated, then you can ask him to step back a pace or two. This is when you look him in the eye and say 'back': be upright in your stance and advance towards him looking him sternly in the eye, and he will usually retreat. If he doesn't, then pinch him on the nerve just above the point of shoulder and again say 'back'. This will make him put his weight backwards and he will find it easy to step back: as soon as he responds to this pinch, lighten the pressure – he will soon learn that when you put your hand towards the point of his shoulder he is expected to step back. Always reward him with a stroke on the neck.

With a colt you must be kind but firm in what you ask him to do: keep him listening to you, and do not allow his attention to wander all over the place as this will shortly be followed by loud and strident whinnying, and this is a very difficult habit to change. Some horses are by nature forward-going and keen, while others seem to 'think backwards' and are thoroughly sluggish in their attitude. These sluggish horses must be made to walk up beside the handler in a businesslike manner, and the handler, too, must be sure to walk in an upright stance and hold himself alertly: this body language is very

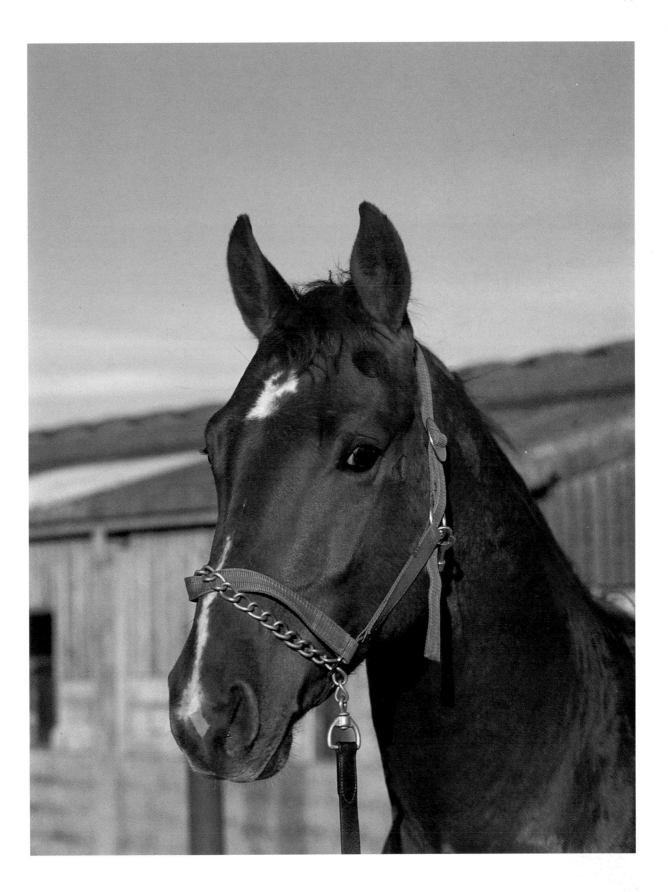

important in all aspects of training.

Before commencing the serious breaking and training of your horse there are a number of things concerning his health and general management that should be done and checked. Some of these may require time off, so it is better to do them before progressing with training; you want to avoid coming up against problems which will force you to break off your programme, disrupting continuity and even nullifying any progress made.

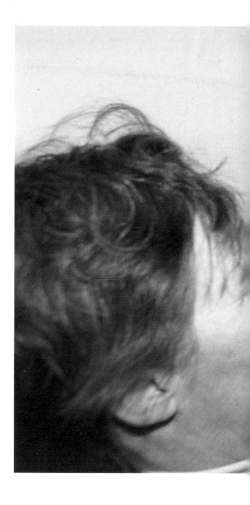

HEALTH AND STABLE MANAGEMENT

Teeth
It is important to have the horse's teeth checked, as any sharp edges should be rasped and wolf teeth may need removing. Wolf teeth do annoy the horse; they move when you come to put a bit in his mouth and the bit touches them, and give the horse some pain. They are usually only found on the upper jaw just in front of the molars, and must not be mistaken for the tushes which appear in virtually every male horse's mouth; these are his fighting teeth and are very deep-rooted, and are situated much lower in the mouth, just below the bit. Thus small wolf teeth do need to come out before bitting; large ones, however, are usually very deep-rooted and will be more of a problem to remove than to leave in. Check also that the baby teeth that should have come out, *have* come out, and that the mouth is fully and correctly equipped.

Worming
A good time to worm a horse is when he comes in to be stabled from running out; think of it as a fresh start with a healthy horse! A horse should be wormed every six to eight weeks when out in the field; when he is stabled he should continue to be wormed, although every twelve weeks should suffice.

Shoes
Before training starts, make sure your horse's feet are trimmed and level so they do not break up once he is in work. You may like to have him shod, although most people

EARLY EDUCATION
It is never time wasted just to lead your horse about and show him the various local sights such as parked cars, your horsebox or trailer and particularly strange obstacles like the dustbin and sacks of feed, to convince him as best you can that they do not bite!

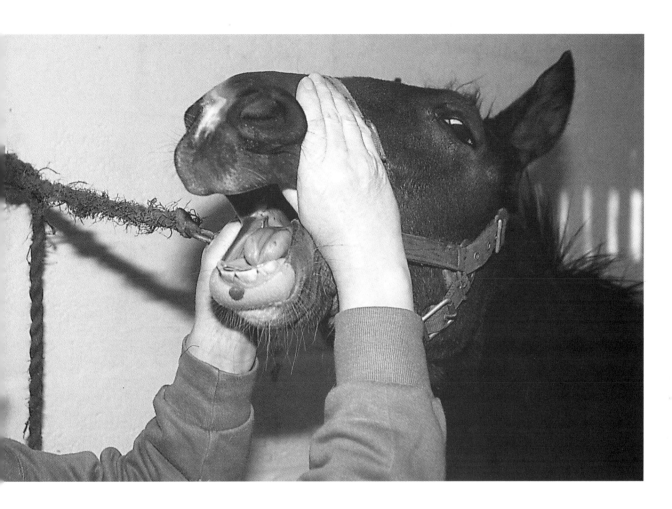

prefer to leave a young horse unshod until he is ready to ride out. For his first set it is preferable to use steel plates or aluminium shoes as these are very light and do not affect his action as much as a heavier shoe might. Ask your farrier whether your horse will take a plate; a big horse with wide feet may need a wider webbed shoe, and this may also be obtainable in aluminium.

Vaccinations
In Britain, every competition or registered horse should have a correct identification document which undeniably relates to the animal concerned. This means that the full picture diagram on it, together with the description supporting the diagram, *must* be

completed, signed and stamped by a veterinary surgeon (who is not the owner of the horse); this document should remain with the animal for the rest of its life, so take care of it! Your horse has to have the following injections at the intervals listed below in order to be eligible to go to all affiliated competitions and many open shows. These dates are based on Jockey Club rules; they are the most frequent, but it does also mean you can stable your horse at any racecourse stables. In the United States you should check with the American Horse Shows Association (AHSA) for competition requirements. Be sure that the vaccinations are not rendered invalid by forgetting to have any one injection within the correct period.

The young horse must learn to allow you to look in his mouth: open it by inserting your fingers and thumb at the bars and then by using light pressure of the thumb towards the roof of his mouth. Normally you would always untie a foal before examining his mouth but, as can be seen here, this particular foal was accustomed to being tied up and handled in this way, therefore it was safe

First injection of the primary vaccination 21 – 92 days' gap (ie the second injection should be given not before 21 days after the first, and not after 92 days after it)
Second injection of the primary vaccination 120 – 180 days' gap
Third injection

From the date of the third injection your horse must have an annual booster *within* one year (365 days) – if you go even one day over the year, or exceed the required number of days between injections, then all of the above will be invalidated and the horse will have to start the whole course of injections right from the beginning again.

Trimming and Clipping
It is advisable to trim your young horse before you start to ride him: if he has a long mane or whiskers they might get caught in the tack and could pull, causing him to fuss and fidget about the head. Besides, a long and matted mane can get caught in your fingers. This is best pulled when the horse is hot and sweating as the pores will then be more open making it much easier to pull out, as well as being less painful for the horse. It is better to do just a little at a time, and only to pull out small bits of hair at a time, too: first back-comb the hair lightly until you have the required amount in your fingers, then pull these out quickly. Trim up the whiskers under the chin and around the elbows, using either

a pair of clippers or a pair of scissors and a comb, and trim the heels at this stage, too, though this rather depends on the time of year: in spring the horse will be getting his summer coat and a lot of his feather will fall out naturally; however, a heavier type will always look more elegant with trimmed heels and they are easier to dry when he is washed off after work. In the autumn and winter he will, of course, sweat quite readily, being unfit and more woolly, and it may be advisable to give him a trace clip so that he doesn't get too hot and sweaty, and thus susceptible to chilling, when he starts work; besides which he is less likely to get girth galls if he is clipped around the girth area.

Some horses are nervous of the clippers, and I would recommend that before you clip your young horse you put him in a stable next to another horse being clipped so he becomes accustomed to the noise and learns that it isn't going to hurt him or affect him in any way. When you come to clip him, start by placing your hand on his shoulder and putting the clippers on your hand so that he can feel the vibration through your hand first. If he is quiet and happy about that, then you can continue and start to clip him. If he is upset by the clippers, the noise or the feel, then you must take things slowly; make sure the clippers don't get hot, as this can upset a sensitive horse. You may like to leave them running for a while, so he can get used to the noise, and then just quietly persevere with holding the clippers on your hand on his shoulder and withers area. Next, gently stroke the clippers up and down the lower half of the neck until the horse accepts this contact with them. Some horses hate to see their hair falling on the ground, apparently believing that

GROOMING
The horse should be quartered and have his feet picked out before he starts exercise each day, and he should be groomed lightly when he has cooled off from work. In this way the young horse becomes used to being handled and brushed, and realises that it is neither a painful nor a frightening experience. Gentle but firm handling is required with a horse which is ticklish or fidgety; this sort must be made to stand still and behave, and although you must take care not to tickle or annoy him, always be firm, and always try to establish a partnership of mutual trust and respect with your horse.

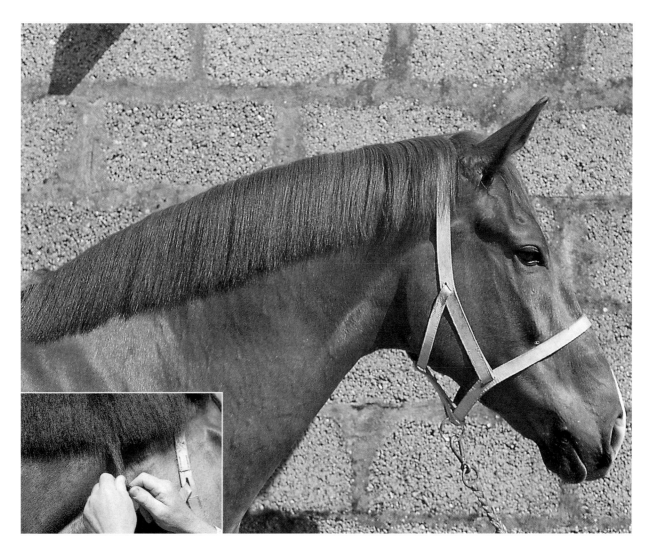

you have cut them; if you can cover their eye for a few minutes they usually relax.

You must be very careful not to nick the skin when clipping near the elbows and between the horse's front legs and hind legs; the skin is very thin here, and they can become very ticklish. Clip all bony parts of the body carefully, too, as the clippers will cut closer where bone, and not soft tissue, is beneath the skin, and you can end up with a skeleton effect! Make sure that your clipper blades are sharp and that they are correctly tensioned; if the tension is wrong the blades will not lie together properly, and then they will just catch the hair between the blades and pull it – this will leave a lasting association in the horse's mind between the noise of the clippers and pain.

When the horse is happily accepting the feel of the clippers you should be able to move the blades over the coat in easy, slowly sweeping strokes, keeping the feel against the skin even at all times so as to make a clean shave. The clippers should be kept cool by frequently rinsing the clipper heads in a pot of paraffin and oil mixed; then wipe off the excess before starting to clip again.

Make sure you never over-pull a mane; manes that are too short will never lie down properly. Aim for a neat, evenly pulled mane, about 4in (10cm) long

Single-ring, three-strap cavesson

Dear Edward correctly dressed for lungeing for the first time, wearing a cavesson, four boots and the lunge rein; I have a lunge whip and am wearing gloves

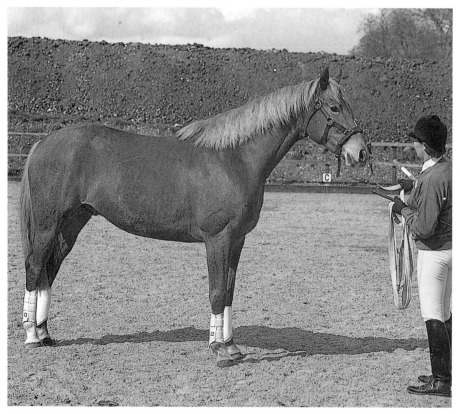

Training on the Lunge

THE OBJECT OF LUNGEING

Lungeing teaches the horse to obey the trainer. It also teaches him to balance himself on a circle but without the unaccustomed weight of the rider, and it builds up his muscles and tendons and tightens the ligaments. Finally the horse learns to respect his trainer through learning to obey the forward driving aids of whip, voice and rein aids; though once the horse understands the voice he can be lunged with virtually the voice alone. Done correctly, lungeing builds up the horse's confidence in his trainer, its pattern of obedience and praise giving him a feeling of security and establishing his trust in his trainer so that when he is ridden he will accept this next stage in his education without stress.

Facilities

A horse can be lunged either loose or on a lunge rein, and if you have a lungeing ring it is much easier as the horse cannot lean on the lunge rein; he is also well enclosed. Otherwise a school of some sort is helpful, or a manège, or a small, well-fenced paddock. If you do not have this sort of facility, then you must teach your horse to lunge correctly on a lunge rein and be able to control him in any place. Good footing is

BASIC EQUIPMENT

The process of training on the lunge can really be considered in two stages; the equipment required for the first stage is as follows:

Cavesson: This can be made of leather or nylon; the noseband is made of steel padded with either leather or nylon, and it has one or three rings to which to attach the lunge rein (left and overleaf). The cavesson should be fitted quite snugly round the horse's head, with the noseband two fingers' width below the cheek-bone; it should be done up quite firmly to stop it slipping round the horse's nose. The cheek-strap should be done up firmly to stop the cheekpieces moving too near the horse's eye; if you have a throatlash this should be done up loosely, allowing three fingers between the cheek-bone and the strap.

Lunge rein (25ft/8m): This is usually made of webbing 1½in (3.8cm) wide; it can also be made of cotton, or nylon. Some people prefer to use plough lines, but I find them too bulky.

Lunge whip (approx 6ft/2m with a lash of 2m): This is used to encourage the horse to move forwards with a light flick on the hind leg when needed, but it must be used in combination with a voice aid. The horse has to be taught that the whip can bite quite sharply if not obeyed, then it only has to be waved in the future.

Exercise boots (four): These can be of any brand, and are used for protection against knocks which the horse might incur from losing his balance as a result of not being accustomed to lungeing or moving on a circle.

Gloves: It is important for the handler to wear gloves because if the horse does pull away then burns may be caused to the hands if they are not protected. It is also important to wear flat shoes or boots.

Cavesson with three rings and two straps

important as you will not get a horse to show his true paces if he is afraid he might slip on a hard or slippery surface; for preference it should be of sand or some artificial fibre.

When loose lungeing in a lungeing ring all you have to do is ask the horse to move away from you with a click with your tongue; give him a small flick with the whip if he does not react straightaway. You can have the horse free, or have a cavesson and lunge line attached, the latter being preferable if you wish to teach the horse to lunge in another place.

The Whip
Used correctly, the horse might consider the whip to be an extended limb of the handler, and one which can kick him   ie give him a sharp flick or a quiet stroke – quite effectively. It should only be used on the hind leg, to encourage forward movement or when making a correction. If the horse cuts in on the circle the whip can be pointed more towards the shoulder so as to push him away from you, making him bend round the circle and the direction of the whip which is then acting as your inside leg. You should only have to use the whip once or twice for the horse to become aware of its exceptional influence. Unfortunately many people use the whip almost as an instrument of torture, and not as an aid. When riding, the whip should reinforce the leg and seat aids, and should be used in conjunction with the voice – ultimately the horse should react immediately to your voice, so that in later life the whip is virtually never needed.

To change the lunge whip from one hand to the other, pass it behind your back so that you don't frighten the horse by inadvertently waving it about when changing hands. In fact, once the horse is trained it is easy to change the whip around as the horse will have complete confidence in you – he will respect the whip, but will have no fear of it if he has been correctly treated.

LUNGEING TECHNIQUE

In the initial lessons some less experienced handlers may find it easier if they have an assistant to start the young horse off; he or she can lead it out on the circle whilst you gradually move in to take up the lunge rein or whip, whichever is preferred. Personally I like to do it alone, as the horse seems to pay attention better when there is only one person for him to attend to.

If your horse leads correctly, then lungeing should be no more than an extension of this process. At the beginning it is always helpful to show any young horse the area you are going to lunge him in; it seems to give him confidence, so I would lead him on the right rein round the area. If he is frightened of anything he will nearly always run to the centre of the area since it is usually empty of any startling objects; if this happens, move yourself quietly to the object that scares him, and in time ask him to come to you. Because you have placed yourself next to the frightening object the horse will come to trust you and look to you for comfort – just as in a herd of horses there is always one which is bold and leads the others, one which by nature is courageous; this is the leader, and he will take the others to objects which they would otherwise be snorting at, and because of this confident attitude the others will then come and explore everything around him. Catherston

Dear Edward lungeing for the very first time, so with only basic lungeing equipment. We have blocked off a part of the school to make a more confined, enclosed area; this helps the young horse to settle

Dance in the Dark was one of these adventurous ones.

This dominant role *you* take on, and therefore you have to be quiet, confident and relaxed in your posture so that your laid-back demeanour will instil confidence in the horse, too.

Having walked the horse a few times round on your lungeing circle, change the rein and walk the other way, so that you have led him from both sides. Gradually let him out on a longer rein, and by changing the rein and whip into the other hand (ie lunge rein in the left hand and whip in the right), you will be in a position to lunge him properly on the left rein. When doing this, remember to change the whip by taking it from your left hand behind

your back with your right hand so that you don't frighten the horse.

The procedure for lungeing on the left rein is as follows: the rein should be held in the left hand, with the remainder of the rein in the right hand, and the whip in the right hand pointing towards the horse's quarters to encourage him forwards should it be necessary. If the horse is moving *too* freely forwards then the whip should follow much further away. As long as the horse continues to walk on a longer rein on a bigger circle that is fine, but sometimes he doesn't and comes back to you; in this case you will have to drive him away from you more positively with a light flick with the whip. You must really allow the horse to move away at whatever speed he takes up, and not try to slow him down until he has got the idea of going forwards. It is important not to be contradictory to the horse, so be sure to separate your commands.

When lungeing the trainer must take care always to be in the correct position to encourage the horse forwards, and must therefore position himself just behind the centre of the horse as it moves round the circle. On the left rein the trainer must follow round with the left leg as pivot, and with the right leg as pivot on the right rein; but having said that, when starting off a young horse you often have to move about a bit to get into the driving position until it has got the idea. Then your inside leg is your bracing leg and your pivot.

As soon as the horse goes forwards and away from you, you must guide him with the lunge rein, the whip and where you stand so that he gets the idea of where he is to go. As soon as you can, reward him with your voice and a lightening of the lunge rein; this indicates to him that he has done well. You must then teach the horse the feel on the lunge rein that ultimately you should both find comfortable; it should be a light feel and not a strong pull, basically the same as you would feel on the reins when you are riding, with the arm bent at the elbow and the hand carried in the same manner. The end of the lunge rein is in the whip hand and can shorten and lengthen as necessary.

Having taught your horse to go forwards on the circle in walk and trot, the next lesson he must learn is to come back to walk, and to whoa or stand. You will have taught the horse basic obedience when leading in hand, so he will know the words of command before you start to lunge him and will probably be glad to listen to something he knows. If he doesn't want to slow down or stop when asked, give him a little time before asking again, as something could have made him lose concentration. If he doesn't slow down to your voice aids and refuses to listen, then you will have to make him: move yourself into his path, pushing him towards the wall with your own eye contact and aggressive stance, and dare him to continue – say 'whoa' at the same time and also shorten up your lunge rein. When he does finally stop, reward him with your voice; then move yourself more towards his quarters so that he goes forwards again. After a few circles ask him to halt again, and follow the same rather aggressive procedure if necessary; if he does listen to you, then reward him with your voice; and if he stands where he was asked, then stop the exercise and reward him with a stroke on the neck, having quietly gathered in the lunge rein.

You must now teach the horse the same lessons on the right rein. Unfortunately, the horse doesn't reason like we do, and just because

PULLING OUT AND CUTTING IN

When lungeing, most horses are inclined to pull out on one part of the circle and to cut in on the other. Vibrate on the lunge rein when the horse pulls on it, and try to teach him that you don't want this strong pressure by keeping on lightening the rein. If a horse tries to cut in, look him in the eye and with your own body language, drive him away from you. If you do this and also point the whip towards his shoulder, he will soon keep out and make a true circle. The worst thing you can do is to step back and away from the horse in order to keep the tension and the length of the rein constant – this just encourages him to cut in more, and is bound to make him feel he has the advantage.

he has learned to lunge on the left rein do not assume that he will automatically do it to the right: he won't. You must first lead him round on the off side, then allow him out on a longer rein; hopefully he will then carry on as he learned to do on the other rein. However, you often find that on the right rein he will move away from you, but then feels unsure of himself, stops, and turns in to look at you. If this happens you must be quick to shorten up your lunge rein and go to his head from the off side; then start all over again. He will undoubtedly try to do the same thing again at the same spot, so you must be quick to drive him forwards *before* he gets to it, so that you actually prevent him from turning in; it is only by your quickness and superior intelligence that you overcome any disobedient habits. If he manages to turn in again then you must reprimand him: 'attack' him with your aggressive stance and send him backwards for several steps so that he realises that he has done wrong. Back him into a corner if possible, and then keeping yourself on his off side, drive him forwards with the whip in your left hand. Allow him to go forwards, remembering where he is likely to turn in again so as to be ready to send him firmly forwards. This repetition is essential in order to teach your horse to respect you, and to maintain his concentration.

When starting a young horse on the lunge, five minutes on each rein is probably enough, although this very much depends on the temperament of each horse – sometimes having learnt to go forwards it takes him a little time to learn to stop! If this is the case, then on the first day it is better to stop when you have achieved a good understanding on just the one rein,

as you must take care not to tire a young horse too much; ten to twelve minutes should be your maximum. When the horse is fitter he would probably manage seven to ten minutes on each rein; a maximum of twenty to thirty minutes, with walk and a rest period before each change of rein, is normal for an experienced horse.

Turning away from you
This is a nasty habit and must be corrected quickly; a normal cavesson is often not quite sharp enough to correct a horse with this habit, so try using a Wells cavesson as this is positioned lower on the nose. If the horse intends to turn away from you he usually gives you some warning, either with his eyes or the way he holds his neck – stiffening the muscles on the inside, for example – and as soon as you see any such indication try some sharp jerks on the lunge rein to change his mind. If they don't and he does turn away from you, then try to halt him and turn him back the same way he turned – thus on the left rein, if he pulled away to the right then pull him back to the left again. If you feel you are not going to get on top of him with the Wells cavesson, then I would use a headcollar with a chain threaded over the nose. This must be fitted so that it releases quickly, and should only be used with a special type of headcollar with rounded dees. I would fit the headcollar and give the horse a smart reminder that you are the boss by giving him a sharp jerk on the lunge rein when he is not paying attention to you, just to make him listen. Then lunge him in the normal way and be ready for any sign of turning away; if possible have an assistant to help stop him should he try to get away. Insist he goes where he is told: whenever he does,

be quick to praise him. Don't go on for too long – get your way and reward him, go on lungeing for a few more circles, then stop and rest.

In one particularly bad case I had to lunge a horse with a chain and a Chifney. This is a very severe measure, but I had to break a long-standing habit and this horse did not wish to feel anything; he was stubborn and pig-headed, and having got away from his owners on many occasions had been sent to us for remedial training. I thought I was forewarned and therefore forearmed, but not a bit of it; he took me and my assistant just where he wanted even with the chain over his nose, and the only other thing I could think of was a bridle with a gag rein over his head – this is very severe, but he still didn't take any notice and seemed to delight in leaning on the rein, which I felt didn't do his mouth any good. It was therefore as a last resort that I sent for the Chifney. We lunged the horse with the chain over his nose and with another rein on the Chifney, and whenever he got strong or tried to pull away I fed him little jerks on the Chifney which changed his mind.

After a few days of lungeing him with the Chifney, and gradually using it less and less, the horse became altogether more obedient and we could dispense with the Chifney and just lunge him with the chain. This he also respected; but I wouldn't lead this horse in just a headcollar or he might have reverted to his old habits. A horse never forgets, so always be aware that if he has once got away with something, there is always the chance he might try to do it again, especially with a new or inexperienced handler. In this case, the *owner* was then taught how to cope with his horse; and finally they both lived happily ever after and came to respect each other and become friends.

BITS AND BITTING

Once your horse is lungeing happily on both reins it is time to get him used to having a bit in his mouth. At this point always check to make sure that he has not got any wolf teeth: if he has, get the vet to remove them unless they are very big ones, in which case they are usually very deep-rooted and won't bother him. The small wolf teeth are like milk teeth and will move when the bit touches them, giving the horse some pain; naturally he will start to look uncomfortable and become worried by the bit.

When introducing a bit to a young horse, take care not to hurt him when putting the bit into his mouth. In a young horse the mucous membrane lining the hard palate of the mouth is very pronounced and in fact lies lower than the upper incisor teeth; thus if he closes his mouth on the bit when it is too low in his mouth it will give him pain. You must therefore make sure that he opens his mouth correctly so you can slip the bit well into his mouth to prevent causing him any discomfort.

With a sensitive young horse it is often helpful to use a light nylon bit and to let him play with it and get used to it being in his mouth in the stable for an hour or so before you intend to work him. In this way he will learn to put his tongue in the correct position; also by playing with it he creates saliva and this ensures that he has a wet mouth, which is always desirable.

If you have a horse which is difficult to bridle you must first try to find out the cause. Is he frightened of you trying to open his

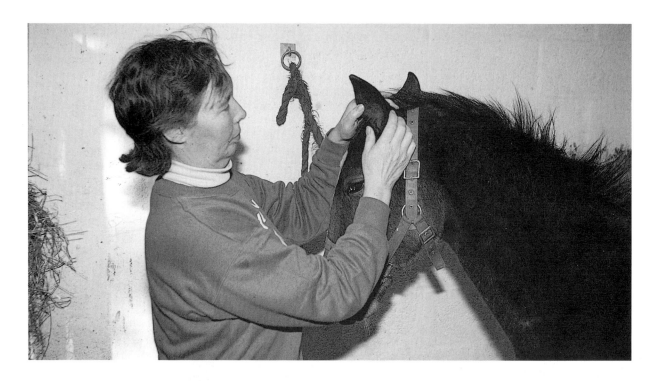

Gently and quietly persuading a foal to allow his ears to be handled

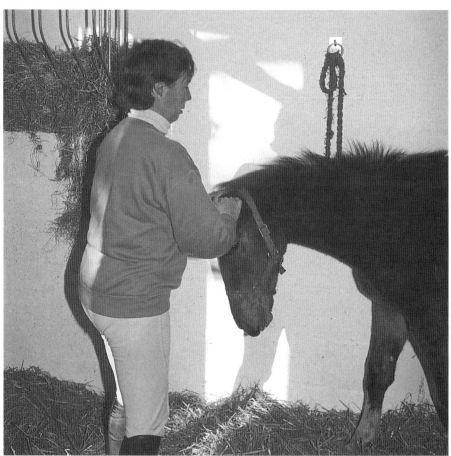

Teaching a foal to lower his head by light pressure on both ears. Remember to untie him first

As soon as he lowers his head, lighten the feel at the base of his ears and stroke them gently

mouth? Is he frightened of you touching his ears? In both cases you must take as much time as is necessary to gain his confidence and correct the trouble, and this should perhaps be done by the same person for some time until the horse is fully accustomed to being bridled and unbridled; a heavy-handed person could so easily undo all the trust that has been built up. Dutch Courage used to be difficult to bridle; I had to stand on a crate as he would put his head up so high I couldn't reach!

Now and again you will have to deal with a horse that puts his head right up and won't let you get your finger into his mouth to open it. Put on a loose-fitting headcollar and position him in the corner of the stable close to the back wall; you will also need a plastic drink crate to stand on. Now put a little honey on the centre of the bit; dip your fingers in a little table salt, and stand up beside the horse's head on the near side. First put your left hand on top of his nose, reassuring him with the other hand. Stroke him all over his head so that he begins to relax and enjoy your presence and the soft stroking around his head. Gradually introduce a finger into the side of his mouth, letting your arms move upwards if he raises his head –

on no account pull down on his mouth. Then push your finger towards the roof of his mouth: this naturally causes him to open his mouth, but when he tastes the salt on your fingers he should actually come to enjoy the experience; let him lick the salty palm of your hand, too – anything to help him find it pleasant.

Once you have got his confidence, you can introduce the bit. The easiest way is to attach one ring of the bit to the off side of the headcollar; then have your assistant place his hand gently on the bridge of the horse's nose and stroke him on the head while you open his mouth with your right hand. With your left hand, slip the bit into his mouth, then attach its other ring to the other side-ring on the headcollar, adjusting the headcollar so that the bit is comfortable in the horse's mouth; it should be high enough so that the lip has a slight wrinkle at the top. You can also give him a small sliver of carrot so that he finds pleasure from having the bit in his mouth.

If a horse is sensitive about his ears then you must teach him that having them handled can be a pleasurable experience, too. This may take several days; and it may also take time to teach him to lower his head when you apply slight pressure on one or both ears – a horse will lower his head almost to the ground if you teach him properly. The drink crate is again advisable so that you can reach as high as he puts his head. Most horses appreciate a little attention – they like to be stroked between the eyes and gently soothed, and their coat scratched lightly with the fingers; so, gradually creep up your horse's head like this and fondle his forelock, taking care not to pull on it – talk to him soothingly and occasionally touch an ear, to start with whichever one appears to be less sensitive. Gently fondle his upper head region until he becomes relaxed and you can then gently stroke the other ear. If he seems shy and tense, don't hold on tight but keep your arm, hand and fingers relaxed, and just go on repeating this treatment for about fifteen minutes a day; gradually the horse will trust you, and eventually you will be able to fondle both ears with both hands.

Once you have reached this stage and won his confidence you could occasionally apply a little downward pressure on both ears and indicate to the horse that you would like his head lower – his natural reaction should be to lower it. However, sometimes he won't, so you have to teach him: thus, as soon as he lowers his head, even a fraction, lighten your feel on his ears and soothingly stroke them until you feel him relax; then apply a little downward pressure again, and so on until you have his trust and relaxation. If you do this correctly you can train your horse to lower his head whenever you stroke his forehead so you can stroke his ears. He is then happy. The next step is to hold your hand out with a sliver of carrot and the bit cupped in your hand so the horse takes both carrot and bit into his mouth; he will have his head low so you can easily put the bridle over his ears.

This sort of initial stable handling makes every horse so much more trusting and easier to deal with. We try to handle our foals every day in the first week so they are used to being touched – they learn to lower their heads and allow you to open their mouths, handle their legs and ears, lift their tails and so on; then even if they are not handled for two or three years the experience is built in, and they never forget that soft

Bits suitable for a novice horse: (on left) loose-ring snaffle, thick eggbutt lightweight snaffle, standard eggbutt; (on right) double-jointed cheek snaffle and a single-jointed snaffle

touch they first learned when they were only a week old. It is such a help later on if you can handle your foal in this way every day; if you don't, they can sometimes become very independent as they grow older, and some appear to become quite wild. However, you can establish these lessons with their dam before weaning; and those that have had their early education very soon come to heel and remember the old routine.

Types of Bit

Once the horse has become accustomed to a bit I usually use one of the following for his daily work:

Lightweight loose-ring jointed snaffle: I find most horses go extremely well in this bit; it is thick in the mouthpiece, and when the horse moves his tongue the bit moves up in the mouth with the tongue.

Eggbutt snaffle: This is a very useful bit, it is mild and cannot pinch the corner of the horse's mouth, and most horses go well in it; however, it does hang lower in the mouth than the loose-ring jointed snaffle.

Cheek snaffle with keepers: This lies higher in the horse's mouth, and doesn't move up and down with the tongue so much; the cheeks prevent any chance of the bit pulling through a young horse's mouth should he be recalcitrant about turning. It doesn't have a very thick mouthpiece, however, so is inclined to be a bit sharper than an eggbutt or lightweight loose-ring snaffle.

Double-jointed snaffle, with or without cheeks: Some horses prefer this, as the nutcracker action is less severe than a bit with a single joint.

Double-jointed ½-moon snaffle: This is useful for a rather mouthy horse or one which draws his tongue back as it gives more room for the tongue.

D-ring snaffle: This bit is good for not pulling through the mouth, but I find it tends to hang rather low in the mouth and can encourage horses to put their tongue over the bit.

Nylon eggbutt in-hand snaffle: This is a mild bit which is useful for getting a horse accustomed to the feel of the bit in his mouth. It is normally used for in-hand work as it is smooth and very light in weight.

MORE ADVANCED LUNGEING

Technique
If a horse has not been used to having a roller on in the stable with a rug, then you must take care when fitting one for breaking, as an adult horse is more likely to object to it; I always use a girth with an elastic

SECOND STAGE EQUIPMENT
Snaffle bridle: This is a mild, straightforward bit to help the horse get used to holding a bit in his mouth without the pressure of side-reins or long-reins.
Roller with rings to attach side-reins and an **elastic girth**: The roller is used to accustom the horse to having a girth on, and later for attaching side-reins. To start with it must be used with a breastgirth or breastplate to prevent it slipping back, because you must be sure to do up the girth only quite loosely, at least until the horse gets used to the feel of the roller. Tighten it gradually. Some horses become very violent when they first feel the roller. I sometimes use a double piece of baler twine instead of a breastgirth as it is less cumbersome for a young horse.
Side-reins: These are made of plain leather or nylon; there are also side-reins made with an elastic gusset or with a rubber ring to allow a bit of give in the rein. I prefer the latter.
Crupper: A padded leather strap which goes under the horse's tail and attaches to the centre of the roller or saddle to prevent either slipping forwards. It is not often used with riding horses as most have a good shoulder and it is not necessary. When first placed on a horse the handler must take care not to get kicked. Stand on the near side, lift the tail and place the end of the tail through the 'V' of the crupper, move the crupper up to the base of the tail making sure there are no hairs caught under it. Then take the long strap down the horse's back and attach it to the roller. For a comfortable fit you should be able to fit the width of your hand between the horse's back and the crupper strap.
Saddle: Any general purpose or flat saddle is good for breaking in a young horse, but you must use a breastplate or breastgirth as well to prevent the saddle slipping back.

insert as this stretches when he blows himself out against it. Before you place the roller on the horse, put on a breastplate or breastgirth (if you do not have either of these some baler twine will do just as well) so that you need only girth the horse up very lightly but without the fear of the roller slipping back and becoming a bucking strap! I have often had horses who were very fearful of anyone ever putting a roller on them again as they have been frightened so much by the experience of the roller slipping back – as soon as they felt it they would try to take off bucking. Of course it is important to be quite firm with these horses, and make them wait and listen to you, and only allow them to walk. In really bad cases I use a restrainer bridle (see page 57), which I now find invaluable with difficult and spoilt horses.

Once you have placed the breastgirth round the horse's neck, have a well padded roller and place it on the horse's back several times, softly and casually, so that he gets used to the feel. Then when you consider he is quite confident, place it again on his back, go to the off side and attach the breastgirth strap through the roller; then return to the near side and put the breastgirth strap through the upper straps of the roller on the near side, and finally do the roller up, stroking the horse all the while under the girth area as you take it under his tummy. Do it up *lightly*, so that it is only just touching him. Then lead the horse forwards – though if he looks apprehensive let him stop, and reassure him. If he is obviously going to misbehave then let him have his buck, just so he realises that nothing is going to hurt him. When he has settled, make him halt, and do up the girth a hole at a time. With a horse that doesn't care at all,

(Left) Arch roller with five loops at different heights in which to place the side-reins. Long-reins would attach to the lower ring between the buckles. (Right) Leather roller with two rings for side-reins. (Far left) Girth sleeve made of mock sheepskin

then you can girth him up a little quicker; but never do a roller up tight, as it can pinch him. You can use a wither pad, but it must be firmly attached to the roller or it will get dislodged with the first few bucks.

After a few days lungeing with a roller and a bridle the horse should learn to carry himself in a better outline, and to get used to the feel of the reins by wearing side-reins. These are made of plain leather, or leather with an elastic insert or rubber ring which allows a certain amount of give in the rein. I prefer the latter for all young horses, and only use plain leather very occasionally for a horse which leans on the rein. To fit side-reins: they need to be about halfway down the horse's rib-cage and attached between the girth straps, or run through a ring if there is one in a suitable place.

When starting a horse with

side-reins I use the outside rein only, and very loosely, and lunge the horse normally; the weight of the side-rein alone will be enough for him to take a light contact to start with. Gradually you introduce the second rein, which should be the same length. When the horse is lungeing happily you can shorten the side-rein, not more than two holes at a time, until he has a light feel on the outside rein when you are lungeing him. Then change the rein, but before doing this, unclip both side-reins while you turn the horse round to face the other way. Again, clip on just the outside side-rein to start with until he is happily going forwards and taking a light contact, then re-introduce the inside side-rein.

This is a safety precaution, because if anything startles the horse and he throws his head up, or if the

side-rein is too tight and he objects, then he only has to let his head go towards it a little to release any tension; and you must lighten all feel on your lunge rein, as it is the contact exerted by the lunge rein which effectively causes the horse to have a feel on the outside side-rein. If possible just drive him forwards gently and he will relax again; but take care that you don't have both side-reins attached too tight because this can easily cause him to panic and rear or even fall over backwards which could do him a lot of harm. So great care and patience must be employed.

Only when a horse is experienced can you place side-reins on him straightaway, and even then always start with them long and shorten them only when he has got used to them. Also, lead him forwards on to the lunge so that he goes smoothly

Dutch Dream, a 3-year-old by Dutch Gold, correctly dressed for a more advanced stage of lungeing, with cavesson and roller plus side-reins attached

into the reins. Take a bit of time, three or four days at least, encouraging the horse to accept a light contact on the side-reins and gradually adjusting them so that he is in a correct outline for his stage of training.

At the same time you can accustom the horse to a saddle. Proceed in just the same way as you did when introducing the horse to a roller: have a breastgirth or breastplate, although now the horse is used to a girth you will be able to girth him up a bit more firmly, which you must do or the saddle could slip even with a breastplate. Few horses really mind a saddle, although those which are difficult with a roller tend to be difficult with a saddle, too, because of its different feel. Most well-handled horses take it all in their stride, however, and never seem to notice either saddle or

girth if they are correctly and gradually girthed up.

Once your horse is accustomed to the saddle and light side-reins you must work towards building up his back muscles so that he is better prepared to take the weight of a rider when you come to backing him. Gradually shorten the side-reins so that he is carrying himself in a good outline, and working from behind into a contact between the lunge rein and the outside side-rein. During this time, and also when you are long-reining, you can accustom the horse to carrying short stirrups, with the irons dangling against his sides and moving around as he moves from one pace to another. This helps him get used to the movement of something down his sides, so he will not find it so strange when at a later stage he is mounted and feels the rider's legs.

Dutch Dream, obviously at a more advanced stage of training on the lunge than Edward, moving freely forwards in a good working trot, accepting a light contact on the side-reins

Make sure that the stirrups are short enough so that they don't hit him on his elbows as he moves. Some horses do object to the feel of the stirrups, but this doesn't usually last long and will probably only be noticed by those which have already been difficult. These awkward ones should be made to go forwards and reprimanded a bit, as they must realise that bucking is not appreciated. A little flick with the whip on the inside hind leg may be necessary if they persist.

Having got past this stage the horse must be taught to engage himself through transitions from trot to walk and walk to trot; do this by using your voice, encouraging the horse to trot with lively active steps, but not too fast – remember you are looking for impulsion and rhythm, not speed. Pace and forward movement is regulated by your contact on the lunge rein, the encouragement given with your voice, and the occasional flick of the whip towards the hind leg or flank if needed. This stage is the beginning of the diagonal aids – inside leg to outside rein – the whip being your leg and the side-rein contact through the lunge line being your hand.

Several days of working the horse with the saddle and side-reins will help in strengthening his back; though the time you take at this stage very much depends on each individual horse as regards both conformation and temperament. With a horse that appears weak in the back, a longer time lungeing him into a good outline will benefit him before you come to mounting him; and the same applies to a nervous or highly strung horse, as this sort will gain in confidence through the repetition of the exercises on the lunge. However, it is not a good idea to go on lungeing for months as the horse will become so fit that you will make it even more difficult for yourself when you come to ride him! Also prolonged lungeing is not good for the joints of a young horse – constantly working on a circle is bound to be a strain to a certain degree. This is why it is so important to lunge a horse on a large circle and steadily, *not*, as is so often seen with a young horse, spinning round at full tilt on a ten-metre circle.

Once the horse has established confidence in the trainer and is working calmly and happily, he is ready to go on to the next stage; this he should do without stress or nervousness.

Difficult Horses

We have had many difficult horses, one bucking so violently with the roller that he lost his footing, but when he got up he continued bucking for another two or three circuits on the lunge before he would settle at all; even after spending several weeks keeping to quiet work with the roller he then tried the same with the saddle. However, we managed to stop him by putting him in a restrainer bridle and making him walk.

TRAINING AIDS

There are many different forms of training aid such as the Chambon, the de Gogue and draw-reins. They all have their uses but I don't use them, except occasionally draw-reins if a horse is particularly hollow in his back and needs a lot of muscle building in his back and neck. If used on the lunge, the draw-reins should come between the horse's front legs, through the bit-rings and be attached to the side of the roller or girth halfway up his rib-cage. This gives the horse the freedom to stretch his neck and head down, but does not allow him to raise it too high. It is vital to introduce draw-reins slowly as, like side-reins, a horse may panic and rear if they are fitted too tightly.

Restrainer bridle, a useful addition for a particularly strong and wayward horse

Another surprise was a mare we had. She was very nervy if touched around the girth area, though otherwise she was quite quiet to handle – she had learnt to lunge very easily and was quite obedient for her little experience. Anyway, we came to putting the roller on her with the breastplate, and an elastic girth with a girth sleeve, and took a lot of time stroking her around the girth area as she appeared rather anxious and fidgety. In spite of the girth being very loose and our being very quiet in our attempt to lead her forwards, she immediately took off like something from the Wild West rodeo, throwing herself everywhere and screaming hysterically. After about ten circuits of the lunge, however, she calmed down and began to settle to an apprehensive trot; and as everything was very loose I stopped her and tightened up the girth two holes. She had another fit but did settle down fairly quickly.

As she was being so hysterical we decided to leave her in the stable all night with the roller on, to help her get used to it, but not a bit of it: in the morning all the tack was in the bed, though at least unbroken! I didn't worry too much about it and thought we would just carry on that day, but she was just as fidgety and went off like an exploding bomb, managing to buck backwards out of the roller and breastplate which came flying down the lunge line at us! I had never seen anything like it before, and it all happened so quickly. But I was not going to be beaten, and sent for a crupper which we proceeded to fit carefully on this mare, making sure it was placed comfortably under her tail and then attaching it to the roller – so now this horse had a breastplate *and* a crupper to keep the roller in place! Well, we had some more rodeo performances, but this time we had her beat, and buck as she would, she could not get out of the equipment! She then gave up and settled to moving on the lunge on both reins in a relaxed trot. By now I thought we really had convinced this horse that we were not going to harm her, and that she would relax and accept our training efforts as something quite normal.

So it was to my dismay that the next day the mare showed signs of a girth gall, and we had to break off training until we could settle the soreness in the elbow region; for a few days we could only loose lunge, all most annoying as we had taken every precaution to prevent this sort of thing happening, even washing the mare off with normal saline solution. Once training resumed we managed to make slow progress by lungeing her in a crupper, gently introducing the side-reins which in fact she accepted quite happily –

THE TICKLISH HORSE

Quiet grooming with your hands, a cactus cloth or a soft body brush can help to settle a ticklish horse. You must be very relaxed so that your movements don't feel jerky, even if he is reacting to your touch. Obviously you must take care that you are standing in a safe position, and not taking unnecessary risks of getting kicked or bitten. Remember it is always most important to have the horse either tied up, or with a long rein passed through the ring in the stable and back to your hand, so that you can keep control of him at all times.

until we came to the saddle part!

Well, I had thought I was forewarned: I had an old saddle, put on a breastplate and fitted the crupper, and used some binder twine round the saddle as it had not got a proper crupper fitting. It looked as if we had the horse really organised, but like a bolt from a gun she shot off with bronco intentions, snapped my geriatric crupper with the second buck and – hey presto! – the saddle was descending over her ears! I couldn't believe it: this horse was making me look a complete beginner! An SOS went out for another crupper, the saddle was replaced, the new crupper attached and the girths done up tighter – and this time we won! Though not without a good battle, I might add. She had a good try bucking, and managed to get the saddle so far forwards that she stirred up the girth galls she had developed earlier when lungeing with the roller.

Again this meant we had to stop putting a girth on her, although she was only sore in one elbow – and she always had a girth sleeve on, too, so it was puzzling how she managed to develop these. When we were able to get started again she was certainly better and more controllable, and although she blew herself out a lot, she did settle down provided you took time to girth her up; but you always had to take care (as you do with any young horse). In the end this mare went very well on the lunge and became extremely obedient, perhaps because I had to be quite firm with her, and not let her take off like a bronco. She learned to respect and trust me, and so was content to listen and wait for her commands.

Catherston Zebedee was home-bred, but unfortunately was not handled much as a foal, and at weaning was sent to a friend for a

couple of years to grow on. Although quiet to catch and lead about he was particularly ticklish and nervous to handle around his legs and in the elbow area. He learned to loose lunge easily and became quite obedient, but when we came to introduce him to the roller, although he didn't mind us putting it on, I knew that when he felt any pressure around his middle he was going to object. This he did in a big way, bucking so violently that he lost his footing and roaring with rage, and it took some time for him to settle down and relax. In the stable we spent a lot of time handling him round the girth area with a cactus cloth, as he couldn't bear to have even a bodybrush in this area; eventually he accepted the feel of the roller without too much fuss, and later a saddle, though only after a similar display of bucking.

It took some time for us really to be able to trust Zebedee when girthing him up, but quiet patience and firmness persuaded him to trust us, so that now he accepts most situations quite sensibly.

Catherston Dance in the Dark as a 3-year-old. Here he looked quite immature and, though a quality horse, he obviously needed time to mature so he did not need much work for another year. At four he still needed more time but came into his own as a late 4-year-old and is enjoying his work as a 5-year-old

Progressive Training from the Ground

Roller and long-rein: the long-rein is made of rolled webbing so it slips through the ring more easily

Long-reining is the next stage of training the young horse from the ground. The principle of long-reining is to educate the horse about steering, forward movement and being driven from behind, thereby teaching him the first principles of the leg aids. It also encourages more engagement of the hind legs so the horse is in a better position to carry the weight of the rider. He becomes a safer ride as he learns to accept reins round his hind legs and along his sides, and is therefore less likely to kick at a rider should the latter have the misfortune to fall and get dragged.

LONG-REINING TECHNIQUE

When first introducing long-reins to a young horse it is advisable to have an assistant to hold him; I always prefer to long-rein a horse in an enclosed area, too, as it would be extremely dangerous should he become frightened and bolt. If this were to happen in the open you have no way of stopping or turning him, and he could then get loose from you and become even more terrified by the flapping reins.

First, the stirrup irons should be level and should hang to just below the saddle flap; secure them either to the girth, or together by means of a strap or string passed under the tummy of the horse. Next, get your assistant to stand on the horse's near side and hold him with the lunge rein attached to the centre ring of the cavesson; put the second lunge rein through the off-side stirrup and attach it to the outside ring of the cavesson. You must now accustom the horse to the feel of the rein along his off side and round his hind legs, so stand behind him at a reasonably safe distance and let the rein gently touch his side. If he appears nervous, take the rein away from his side, then re-introduce it, and do this many times. Your assistant should keep a close watch on the horse, on his eyes and ears, and on what the trainer is doing; he must reassure the horse and make him stand still.

When the horse is confidently accepting the feel of the outside lunge rein against his hind leg, try taking a couple of strides forwards in walk, and then halt again. If you repeat this exercise several times

successfully, then halt and shorten the outside rein, place the end over the saddle and proceed to the near side. Take the end of the outside lunge rein and allow it to lie on top of the horse's croup near to the tail. Ask your assistant to lead the horse forwards in walk and gradually let him out on to the lunge circle; at the same time let out the lunge rein and come to the centre of the circle. When the horse is walking quietly on the circle you can allow the outside lunge rein to drop over his tail; he may find the feel of the rein strange and may increase his speed, and even kick several times and clamp his tail. However, do not panic or pull on the outside rein,

BASIC EQUIPMENT FOR LONG-REINING

Saddle with irons and leathers: The irons should come just below the saddle flap, and should be tied together under the horse's stomach with the string or strap lying neatly over the girth.
Bridle: Snaffle bridle, with cavesson noseband if the full cavesson is not being used.
Cavesson (three rings): As for lungeing (p 41).
Two lunge lines: As for lungeing, as long as possible and smooth, without knots or repairs.
Exercise boots (four): As for lungeing (p 41).
Lunge whip: As for lungeing (p 41).
Gloves: As for lungeing (p 41).
Assistant wearing gloves.

Girths (from left): elastic webbing; lampwick; mock sheepskin girth sleeve

Humbug being introduced to long-reins, and showing some objection as the rein touches his hind leg. The stirrups are tied down in readiness to introduce the inside long-rein, when the horse is a little more relaxed, having been lunged in a circle

just keep it high enough so that it stays above his hocks. Allow him to settle, which he will do after a few circuits provided you move with him and reassure him. Gradually you will be able to take a slight contact on the outside rein; hold it for a moment only, then release it. With practice and your voice you can take a slight contact on the outside rein when asking the horse for a downward transition. As soon as he responds you must release the outside rein and reward him with your voice.

Having accustomed the horse to the long-rein on his right side, then the same procedure should be

followed when you change the rein. When the horse is confident on both reins you can attach the lunge reins to the bit and gradually move yourself to a position behind him; your assistant could then help you start off by leading the horse with a short rein on the cavesson until he has become accustomed to the feel of both long-reins as you change direction. At this stage you have each lunge rein going through each stirrup. Once the horse is confident in walk with an assistant you could see how he managed on his own: ask him to trot on a circle, working on transitions to and from walk, with your voice and a light pressure on the outside rein. As soon as the horse responds to the downward transition you must reward him with a lightening of the reins. If when you ask for the transition he resists and throws his head about, this generally means you are too heavy-handed and must lighten your feel on the reins. Repeat the exercises and transitions until both you and the horse have arrived at a feeling which you can both appreciate as a pleasant working relationship and so he better understands what is correct and pleasant.

The transition to halt is important, and from this you can also teach the aids to rein back. Teach your horse to walk around the arena and to halt. If he is fidgety, get your assistant to walk beside him; when you ask for halt and he responds, lighten the rein contact and get your assistant to give him a little grass straightaway as a reward. Repeat the exercise until the horse is waiting for his grass. Then ask him to step back a few steps, by pushing him up to the rein with the voice and with a click of the tongue, and then saying 'Back' and not allowing him forwards with the reins. As soon as he takes even one step back, reward him with a lightening of the reins and with your voice, such as 'Good boy'. If he resists and doesn't understand, then get your assistant to help by pinching him on the nerve at the base of the neck and at the same time saying 'Back'. Repeat the exercise several times until he understands. It is much easier for the horse to learn to go back without carrying the weight of a rider, and I find it does help when you wish him to rein back when mounted, as he already understands what you require of him.

The disadvantages of long-reining are that if it is done badly, dangerously or before the horse is ready, it can result in many serious problems, with the horse never trusting you, and sometimes becoming dead in his mouth and putting his tongue over the bit because he feels too much weight in the reins – in other words the handler is too heavy-handed; remember there is far more leverage and therefore pressure on the mouth with long-reins. If this does happen then you should place the reins onto the noseband and through the rings of the bit. The noseband will have to be quite loose, but it does prevent there being excessive pressure on the horse's mouth. The handler must also make sure that the lightness of his hands is more acceptable to the horse. If the horse falls behind the bit then he must be driven up to the bridle with both reins and a touch with the lunge whip if necessary, as well as your voice commands.

As already mentioned, I always prefer to long-rein horses in an enclosed area, as it is extremely dangerous should a horse become frightened and bolt. If this happens in the open you have no way of stopping or turning it – it could then get loose from you and could gallop off onto the road, into parked vehicles and so on with the reins flapping or wrapped round its legs, and psychologically this could scar it for life – flapping ring ropes, flags

NERVOUS HORSES

Catherston Zebedee used to tuck in his tail quite a lot when he was first introduced to long-reins, and was very nervous of changing the rein; it was several days before he would settle and relax when changing from one rein to the other. He also found it difficult to understand that you could sometimes be seen on one side of him, and then on the other; but with patience and quiet handling he settled down and enjoyed his work.

and flapping tents might always remind it of that terrible day. In an enclosed area the situation is not nearly so drastic, as you and your assistant can quickly and quietly control the horse, and catch him before he comes to any harm.

Thus unless I am really confident I do not long-rein outside an arena because of the dangers noted above; if the horse is going well, obediently and quietly I will perhaps long-rein him around the yard and drives in order for him to see some new objects. It is advisable initially to have an assistant walking by the horse's shoulder to lead him if necessary, and just to be there should the horse try to turn round. If he is nervous of a certain object, don't make a fuss, or hurry him or get cross, just allow him time to look and assess the situation before

you ask him to go forwards at his own distance from the object. You could then come round again and ask him to go past the same object again, and if he is good this time praise him well. This will build up a rapport between you and the horse in that when he arrives at a situation which frightens him and you ask him to go forwards he will have learned to trust you and your decisions and will respond by doing so.

TROTTING POLES ON THE LUNGE

Poles on the ground are an excellent introduction to jumping for every horse, besides being an educational exercise; they will also help horses who lack rhythm and length of

Long-reining: the horse is moving forwards freely, and is accepting the rein aids readily

stride in trot. We found this very helpful with Catherston Zebedee who was quite timid and was therefore rather tight in his action. After a time he learnt to relax, and by using the poles both on the lunge and when ridden, he picked up a better rhythm in the trot. First remove the side-reins, then lead the horse over a single pole on the ground. Then place three poles in a curve at a distance of 1.30m (4ft 3in) to 1.35m (4ft 6in), and again lead the horse over the poles. When you commence lungeing, allow the horse to trot over the poles keeping him in the middle of the curve; as he becomes more confident you can push him towards the outside of the curve, therefore encouraging him to lengthen his stride. It is helpful to have an assistant to move the poles and make them a little bit wider as the horse becomes more relaxed. As the horse becomes bolder you can increase the number of poles, therefore helping him to balance and use his limbs with more elasticity. This exercise will also be used at a later stage, when the horse is being ridden.

For a horse which is rather hollow in the back and lacks back muscle you can at this stage introduce long side-reins; this encourages him to seek the rein and to use his back and neck muscles. You can also raise the inside ends of the poles by placing them on hollowed out logs or blocks at their lowest level, which will encourage the horse to work with higher movement and greater activity.

Do not overdo this work with young horses, however, as their joints are not fully hardened until they are five years old. Never use two or four poles as a horse is tempted to jump in and out of them, or even to stand off and jump the whole lot!

PROBLEM SOLVING

Some horses try to turn away from the handler, and this tendency must be quickly apprehended as it could lead to him pulling away out of control and getting loose or kicking back. This situation must not be allowed to happen, and if it should, it is advisable to fit a bridle or even a restrainer bridle on the horse. Lower the jump, and lunge him on a circle just inside the running rail of the jump. Once you have control, move the horse to the fence with the whip close behind him, following his forward movement and giving him the freedom to jump. Always praise him when you get your way, even give him a titbit.

Cutting inside the jump is a naughty habit and you must be quick to correct it: point the whip towards his shoulder and possibly in the girth area, too, and move yourself more towards the wing of the jump. Your position is very important to the horse so that he knows when he is to come on the circle near the fence, and when you want him actually to jump it.

JUMPING SMALL FENCES ON THE LUNGE

This exercise is in logical progression from trotting poles. Start with a small cross-bar, using blocks as the wing on the inside so that the lunge line does not get caught up, and have a side pole as a running pole for the lunge line to run over; this will also act well as a wing. Lay a placing pole on the ground 2.5m (8ft) in front of the cross-bar. If the horse has not already experienced trotting poles then I would lead him over some poles on the ground and past the wings so he is used to where you are going to lunge him. He should then be lunged in the normal way and asked just to pop over the obstacle in a forward manner.

Having trotted him over the poles and jumped the cross-bar a few times, you can raise the cross-bar in height, or introduce a third rail, thus making an easy ascending oxer. Next you could introduce a front vertical rail, making it into a parallel. The height of the fence depends on the natural ability of the horse; some will pop over 1m (3ft), whilst for others 0.5m (18in) is ample – in fact it is better to make the fence wider than to make it too high. The placing pole helps the horse to take the fence on a good stride – as he becomes more accustomed to jumping, however, you could try removing the placing pole so he has to work it out for himself. Catherston Dazzler showed exceptional ability and boldness over fences as a three-year-old, whereas Catherston Zebedee was more timid, and showed his natural carefulness.

When jumping a horse on the lunge you must be sure that you move *with* him as he jumps, and not pull him round on a short circle as he lands because this will upset his natural bascule, or roundness, and will also put a lot of strain on the inside hock and fetlock joint; it is vital to follow the horse, and to bring him round on the circle gradually. Thus the degree of contact on the lunge rein is important as the horse must have complete freedom of his head and neck when he is in the air over the jump – on no account should he receive a painful jab from the lunge rein.

EQUIPMENT

It is essential to dress a horse in protective boots for loose jumping: the front legs must be protected with tendon boots, and overreach boots are essential. The saddle can be put on, without stirrups but with a breastplate and preferably surcingle (over the saddle) to keep the saddle flaps down. If a bridle is used, take the reins off.

LOOSE JUMPING

Jumping loose in a jumping lane is of great advantage to most horses: it gives the trainer the chance to see a horse's natural ability and style; it teaches the horse to look after himself, to think, and to look at what he is doing; it helps the horse to regulate his stride because the distances between fences can be altered; and it teaches the horse a better jumping technique without the difficulties inherent in lungeing on a circle. Once a horse enjoys his jumping he will continue to jump a line of fences without the help of an assistant to lead him and start him off, and much progress can be made with you just moving appropriately round the school with a reward in a bucket. To begin with, however, you will need at least two assistants.

Loose jumping is most safely carried out in an indoor school or a fenced outdoor arena. The jumping lane should start with a wider, funnel-type entrance coming out of the corner, its inner fence constructed with poles at about 1.30m (4ft 3in) in height; unless the lane runs right round the school, the barrier at the end of the lane to stop the horse should be the arena rails or a high gate; one assistant should stand there holding a bucket of nuts or oats to reward the horse. This person should be very quick and alert, as young horses which feel they have done a good job – or if they got a smack! – often leap and jump around, sometimes kicking and rearing. Some horses – Zebedee, Humbug and Dance in the Dark, for example – learn to come down the lane and go straight to the bucket, others are inclined to get over-excited and have to be carefully handled by the person leading into the lane and by the catcher. There

should be plenty of room between the last jump and the end of the lane so the horse does not have to stop short after jumping; the lane could be brought round the top end of the school to come up against the other long side if extra space is needed.

When starting a young horse, just put out a placing pole 2.5m (8ft) from where the first fence is to be, and put the two poles which are to make your first fence on the ground; lead your horse over the poles in walk, take him to the end of the lane and give him his reward. Then

let him out of the lane. Next time come down in trot on the lead-rein with an assistant following behind with the lunge whip; if all goes well you can then make a small cross-bar and let the horse go down the lane loose. The first few times you may have to follow him quite closely with the whip to get him to go by himself.

Your handler should lead the horse with a short, plain leather strap, threaded through both rings of the bit or the bit and noseband (depending how strong the horse is) and doubled back; once the horse is

Catherston Zebedee loose jumping with ease and great confidence

This horse is showing good jumping over a sizeable fence in the indoor arena. I would always prefer to see a horse loose jumping in a headcollar or bridle, and with overreach boots

going forwards into the lane the handler should let go of one end of the strap, making sure the loose end does not flap as it comes free and hit the horse around the face. Once the horse has got the idea you can add a second jump 6 to 7m (20 to 23ft) from the first, depending on his size and the length of his stride; it should be a vertical to start with, but can have the back bar added to make a parallel as the horse becomes bolder.

The size of the obstacles very much depends on the horse's natural aptitude and ability. You would be very satisfied if the horse were jumping 1m (3ft) at the end of his

first attempt at loose jumping, though a more timid horse may find 0.5m (18in) sufficient for the first occasion. It is very much a question of weighing up the boldness and temperament of the horse when loose schooling, as a good natural jumper will quickly get bored and careless unless he has something more substantial and interesting to jump; for these you may need to use fillers on your second or third occasion. Zebedee and Dance in the Dark certainly enjoy a challenge.

An important step in the horse's education is to vary the distances – you could have, say, a bounce fence at the beginning (2.8 to 3m/9½ to

10ft between the fences) followed by either a one-stride combination (6 to 7m/20 to 23ft) or a two-stride combination (9 to 10m/30 to 33ft initially). This also provides variation and interest. The distances between the fences can be increased as the horse becomes more fluent, from 7 to 7.6m (23 to 25ft) for a single stride and 10 to 10.6m (33 to 35ft) for two strides, or possibly 11m (36ft) for a big-striding horse. Shorter and longer distances can be set to achieve certain objectives in training the horse: short distances will oblige him to shorten his stride and come closer to his fences and thus use his back, shoulders and forelegs more effectively; longer distances can be set for a horse that jumps rather too high, or for one that does not go forward to his fences enough. However, in the early stages it is important to gain the horse's confidence, and only then can you start altering the distances to make him think for himself.

Some horses get over-excited and jump too fast, taking out strides, jumping very flat, even crashing through fences and therefore frightening themselves. It is often possible to overcome this by careful schooling and use of distances down a lane; try putting in extra poles on the ground to make the horse take the correct number of strides. However, it does take a lot of time and patience to regain a horse's confidence in the jumping lane, and you need to start with small fences again to reassure the horse that he can cope.

With a lazy animal, loose jumping can be very beneficial as he has to motivate himself to make the distances in the line of fences, particularly if they are set slightly long; this can be reinforced by the assistant using the whip on the hind leg on the approach to one or more

> **BE CAREFUL . . .**
> Take care never to over-jump horses when loose schooling; it is very easy to get carried away, especially with a good horse, and he should only be asked to jump down the lane between three and five times in one day. He should be rewarded, and walked round quietly for a few minutes between each session.

of the fences. However, please impress upon all helpers that the whip should *never* be used on the horse as he is taking off over a fence, as this will distract his attention and could prevent him concentrating on the fence he is jumping. Ideally you should have assistants placed in between the fences, and they must be instructed *not to use the whip* until the horse has passed them, as their movement will almost certainly distract its attention.

Build up the fences, ideally starting from the last fence; however, you can also build up from the first if the horse is rushing, or put something more substantial like a filler to make it look at the fence and pay attention to what is in front of it. It is also important to keep the horse interested by altering the appearance of the fences.

A horse that refuses at any fence should be caught and quietly taken out of the lane and started again, the obstacles having been lowered; you could even put just some poles on the ground so that initially he can go down the lane without any likelihood of problems. But the assistant must be ready to use the whip if necessary to make the horse pop over the poles, and this exercise should be repeated until the horse is going down the lane freely by himself, getting his reward at the end.

All the horses we have loose schooled have really enjoyed it once they understood what was required of them, the only exception being Dutch Gold who will jump anything on the lunge or ridden, but has absolutely no confidence if he is not physically attached to a human. He hated being loose schooled, and could hardly manage to move away from the leader and over the first fence! We decided not to persevere with loose schooling him as he so obviously didn't enjoy it, and his style and ability were so good on the lunge and ridden that there was really nothing further to prove, except that it upset him! Most of our young horses that have been loose schooled can be let loose once they are shown the bucket and the jumping lane, and will go and jump down the line of fences of their own accord until they are told to 'whoa' – then they go straight to the bucket for their reward!

Loose jumping outside: this is a safe obstacle, with plastic wings and a low guide rail. This horse is correctly dressed with overreach boots and bandages on his front legs, and is wearing a headcollar so that he is easy to catch and lead

BACKING

Backing should be no more than an extension of your handling, and by now the horse should be quite accustomed to you doing odd things with it! We like to start by giving the rider a leg-up so that she or he just lies across the saddle; in this way the horse can become accustomed to the weight on his back. It is important to choose a light and agile rider, and preferably an experienced one; it is also important to have a knowledgeable person controlling the horse, and an assistant to give the rider a leg-up. Before starting it is imperative that you check all the tack to be sure the saddle will not slip, and that the holder has control and will be able to stop the horse should it panic and shoot off. A breastplate or neck-strap

is often a help to the rider as something to hold on to if the horse becomes tense.

Use the middle of the school or arena, and be sure there are no scattered poles or unsafe objects should the rider be deposited or for the handlers to trip over; also make sure that there are no dogs, children or any other distraction which could upset a young horse. Stand the horse in the centre of the school; you then have room to move him a few steps at a time without having to turn sharply. Get the assistant to give the rider a leg-up across the saddle, making the horse stand and reassuring him; repeat this exercise several times until he appears relaxed and settled. You can do this from both sides, though be sure you all change sides. When the horse seems confident and quite unconcerned, you can move him one or two steps, and halt again. Gradually the rider could hold himself in a more upright position so that the horse sees the rider rather higher behind him; lead the horse for a few more steps, and stop. You can repeat this until you consider the horse confident. Next, dismount the rider, then give him a leg-up so he sits correctly on the horse; he must be very careful that his leg does not brush its hindquarters, and that he lands quietly and lightly in the saddle. Repeat the moving and halting exercise; if the horse looks in the least bit apprehensive you must stop him immediately and reassure him – in this instance it may be sensible to let the rider dismount and mount many more times before moving again.

It is always better to do only a little at a time; just leading at the walk may be all you do on the first day you mount. With another horse, however, you may be able to go much more quickly, and even have

MOUNTING PROBLEMS

We had one Anglo Arab colt to break in which used to lie down and try to bite you when you put your foot in the stirrup. He was very ticklish, and this problem was the result of someone having poked him in the ribs when trying to mount. In fact it was quite funny, because whenever you tried to put your foot in the stirrup, the horse went down on his side snapping like a dog! We managed eventually to get on him with a leg-up, and he was not the least bit fearful of the rider, though when dismounting he became very agitated by the loose stirrups. On day one we therefore just mounted and dismounted a lot, always with a leg-up. After a few days of riding him he was more confident in his rider so we were able to progress to mounting from a block – just stepping on and off, never letting either stirrup or foot get near his elbow or tummy. After a few days we were able to dispense with the block; he had become quiet, and obviously confident that we were not going to hurt him in any way, and ultimately he became a good riding horse when we explained to the owners the precautions they would have to take when mounting him.

the rider walking and trotting on the lunge the first day he sits on it. Be firm, even with more nervy horses, and don't let these ones fool you into believing that they are totally frightened. With a very highly strung horse, or one that tries to run off whenever you mount, it is easier to stand him in the corner of the arena or school and use the walls to help stop him moving. We had to do this with Catherston Zebedee who at the slightest move would try to run off and buck. I had to be very firm with him and *made* him stand on command with my voice and with help from the restrainer bridle, as he would try to run through us and had to learn that this behaviour was not allowed. Within three days he had decided that we were not hurting him, and henceforth accepted his rider and settled down quite quickly; he was

Backing the young horse

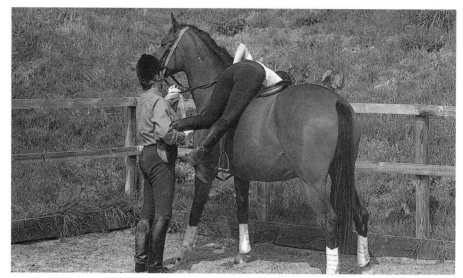

First, leg up the jockey to lean across the saddle so that the horse gets used to the weight without an upright rider on its back

When giving a leg-up make sure that the rider is well clear of the saddle

The rider must arrive slowly and gently in the saddle

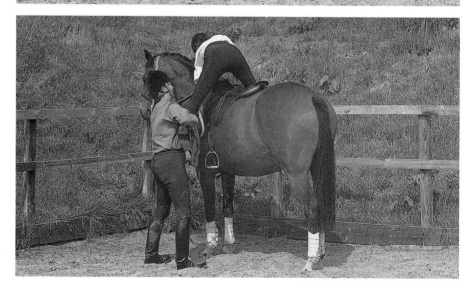

Put the rider's feet into the stirrups so that her feet are clear of the horse's elbows, and so not irritating him

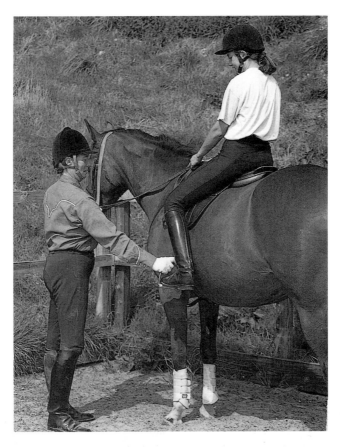

Move just one step and reassure the horse. With a nervous horse it is best to mount and dismount again several times before going on

The horse appears happy and confident, so lead him around a little. But keep a close eye on him so that you can stop the minute he becomes tense

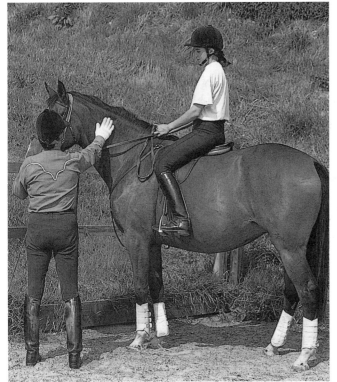

soon out on the lunge. However, he did take quite a long time really to relax with a rider and in his ridden work; a lot of fiddling around with him helped, just stopping, starting and reassuring him.

RIDING THE NEWLY BACKED YOUNGSTER

When riding a young horse for the first time the rider must allow his legs to fold around the horse gradually; he must not clamp them to the horse's side as soon as he gets

on. It is important that the rider is able to relax and move with the horse, in complete balance. As the horse gains in confidence the transitions should be practised, the rider using his voice and giving the commands the horse will recognise, and using his seat and leg aids for upward and downward transitions. The reins should be held in the normal way, with the legs quietly and tactfully riding the horse up to the contact. Because the horse has been trained with side-reins he will immediately carry himself correctly, and should have a light and

Recently backed 3-year-old by Dutch Gold, moving forwards freely and confidently when asked in a strange arena

responsive mouth.

Next the rider can progress to steering the horse, changing the rein within the circle on the lunge for example, and going in the other direction, through walk. The lunger should help the turning by taking a feel on the lunge rein, and stepping back to give the horse room to change direction. If this is done several times and the horse is happy, he can be let off the lunge and ridden in walk around the arena. The lunger can help move the horse in different directions by moving himself around the arena, pushing it

forwards and away from him, and perhaps just following with the lunge whip if needed.

The rider can move the horse forwards into trot, and circle in trot and change the rein. Sometimes it is a help to have a schoolmaster horse to give the youngster 'a hand', but ultimately he has to learn to go where he is asked on his own, and to steer – though this should not be a problem if he has done a little long-reining. You will find that the horse progresses extremely quickly, and by the end of a week you should be able to ride him out around the local farm tracks and lanes.

At the end of every lesson the rider should dismount quietly and smoothly, taking care not to tickle the horse in the elbows when releasing his stirrups, or thumping him on the neck with head or shoulders, or catching the back of the saddle or his quarters with his leg; his weight should be put on the points or pommel of the saddle whilst swinging the leg over the cantle. The horse must learn to stand without the aid of the handler. Mounting from the ground (as opposed to having a leg-up) is best practised at the end of the lesson when the horse is quieter, having worked and therefore (one hopes) being content to stand still. Firstly use a block to mount with an assistant holding the horse; then progress to the assistant being there but not holding the horse. Mount and dismount as often as is necessary to ensure complete confidence and obedience. The rider must be sure that in no way does he interfere with the horse's sides or elbow when mounting; so many horses have been upset by bad experiences when mounting, experiences which have made them virtually unridable.

Chapter 5

First Stages in Riding the Young Horse

So you have backed your horse and are riding him: now you have to educate him in all the new lessons to be learnt in his life. First he must understand that he has to go forwards in response to the leg and seat aids of his rider; he must accept the rein; then he must learn to balance himself and the rider. He has to be able to follow the directional aids, to be obedient through upward and downward transitions, and to cope with different terrain. He must be helped to get stronger physically so that he can manoeuvre himself and his rider with greater agility and suppleness and so become a confident and obedient ride.

OBEDIENCE TRAINING

Lungeing and long-reining have already instilled the basic principles of the diagonal aids: inside leg to create impulsion, into the outside rein which balances and controls the impulsion, the inside rein in conjunction with the outside leg to direct and control the bend of the horse. However, the first essential is to ride the horse forwards in a straight line down the 'tunnel' of the reins, with the horse accepting a light contact. The contact you use must be acceptable both to you as rider and to the horse: it should not be a vice-like grip on the reins, nor

should there be tension in the rider's arms. This sort of feel on the reins will create violent resistance in the horse and cause him to throw his head about, suck up his tongue or stick it out, open his mouth and eventually get his tongue over the bit – he will be altogether a very unhappy horse.

It is the rider's responsibility to teach the horse good behaviour, and the first step is to use the voice which from his lungeing lessons the horse associates with upward and downward transitions. Thus the rider must use his leg, seat and rein aids in conjunction with his voice so that the horse learns what these signify; and immediately the horse performs a transition when asked, the leg, seat and hand aids must be relaxed – this is the horse's 'reward', so he understands that he has been good and that you are pleased with him. The rider may need to carry a schooling whip, because if the horse does not understand what to do when legs and seat are applied, a touch with the whip *at the same time* as the voice command will reinforce the aid for forward transitions.

If you ask for a transition from trot to walk at the same place, the horse will begin to anticipate this and will come back to walk at that spot of his own volition. You are then in a position to ride into a 'forward' downward transition, and will not have to use the reins to stop as the horse is already offering the movement you require; if you repeat this a few times the horse will soon learn that when you sit more upright in the saddle and gently close your legs, you mean him to slow down. This means he is less likely to show resistance in his mouth in a downward transition, and will keep a 'round' shape. Praise the horse; sometimes allow him to steady a little bit, but then ride him forwards with forward riding aids of seat and legs: this is the start of teaching the horse the **half-halt**, and the half-halt is the foundation of all your transitions, the fundamental means whereby you balance your horse for all future movements, and one which you are constantly perfecting and practising – some form of half-halt is given before any movement is performed, be it turn, circle or upward or downward transition.

The 'forward driving aids' are simply quicker leg aids together with bodyweight, the influence of which moves the horse forwards; when the desired pace is achieved, the rider should be able to move 'with' the horse harmoniously in an upright position. Only when the rider himself is balanced can he balance and control a horse effectively; a horse is an extremely quick animal, and can start, stop and turn very quickly – the rider must therefore be quick himself to anticipate when his horse might react violently, and must remain in balance with the horse should it behave in such a fashion. So much damage can be done if a horse gets away with a situation, such as turning away from a circle because you have been thrown off balance and have temporarily lost control. The next time you try to make that circle the horse is certain to try and do the same thing again, but this time with more vigour – so

TEACHING TRANSITIONS

When teaching the horse transitions (either upwards or downwards) you lighten the aids as a reward, but don't just then flop along with no contact at all; ride the horse up to the rein so that you have a light comfortable feel in your hands, and with your upright body position keep the horse moving forward up to the contact. Your bodyweight and balance give the horse as many signals as your hands.

you must be better prepared to overcome the misdemeanour you allowed to happen the first time. Undoubtedly we have all been caught in this way, but it is only by correcting mistakes quickly that a rider will get true respect and obedience from his horse.

Teaching the horse to make turns and circles is one way of making him obedient to the aids. The moment he responds to a directional aid you must reward him by a lightening and easing of the aids, so he understands that he is doing what you want. This does not mean that you should ride the horse constantly in circles, as this is not good for his physique; however, it is much easier to keep a horse balanced when he is on a large circle than it is to ride him in a straight line. Both should be practised, but when you come from a circle to a straight line you must ride the horse very positively, just as if you were accelerating a car away from a corner.

This is also the beginning of teaching the horse to lengthen and shorten his strides: you come from the control of the circle to ride forwards onto the straight line, and therefore increasing the impulsion; you will then collect this energy again when you use a half-halt to prepare for the next turn or circle. A useful exercise is to increase the length of the strides on the long sides of the arena, then as you

Recently backed 3-year-old by Dutch Gold, establishing a good rhythm in the paces

approach the corner use the half-halt to balance the horse with the outside rein and inside leg, sitting up to prepare him and shorten him so he can negotiate the corner or a smaller circle more easily; a circle will make the horse collect himself quite considerably, and then you ride forwards again on the short side. If you repeat this exercise a few times the horse will learn to collect himself when he feels the half-halts, and to extend the steps in response to your forward riding aids.

Once you have achieved balance and a bit of collection in this way, you must also be sure that the horse will go in a straight line in the same pace, without increasing the strides.

Keep the horse together with your seat and legs, gently riding him forwards and keeping him in balance with a light restraining rein. When he is balanced and going at a speed you both feel happy with, lighten the rein contact by giving and re-taking the reins over a few strides; this can be done quite a lot when schooling a horse, to give him the idea of carrying himself.

The same exercise can be done in canter. However, most horses will at some time fall out of canter when ridden on a straight line, and although you can often prevent this happening by being quick to push the horse forward and up to the rein, in time you will find that you are riding more and more, and the horse is doing less and less. This can be dealt with as follows: when he falls into trot when you haven't asked him, make him halt and stand; wait for him to relax his jaw and to concentrate, by holding him with your legs and pushing him up to the rein – as soon as he relaxes his jaw, relax the rein, walk forwards for a few steps and then go straight into canter again. He must realise that he must stay in the pace you put him in until told to do otherwise, and repeating the halt transitions will make him realise that it is easier to stay in the canter than having to perform rather abrupt transitions again and again.

Sometimes the horse becomes strong in the hand because of your efforts to steady and balance him; in this instance it is often better to ride with a slightly more forward seat, balancing your weight on your stirrups with your seat sitting lightly in the saddle and your shoulders slightly in front of your hips, as this allows the horse to use his back more easily. Persuade him to take less of a hold as follows: stay in balance and give the restraining aids of lower leg and rein, and as soon as he responds, lighten both the rein and leg aids – he will soon get the idea of keeping a lighter feel on the reins in canter. As he responds, so you can regain your normal upright position.

Introducing turns and circles within the paces. The horse is accepting a light contact on the reins and is obedient to the aids

Riding Out

Once the horse has got to this stage it is time he was ridden outside the arena and shown the local sights, with plenty of freedom to go forwards in a straight line; riding him round a field or the farm will educate him tremendously to being obedient and balanced in the wide open spaces. He has to become more mature both physically and mentally, and this may take many months; therefore it is important to work out a fitness programme, and get his muscles stronger: ride him on uphill inclines, teach him also to trot downhill, and to canter up- and downhill in a balanced manner in just the same way as you started in your arena. Some horses will by nature be more excitable and have a lot more natural impulsion, and this should be exploited to help you lengthen the strides: thus allow him to go freely forwards in trot, then ask him, with half-halts, to come back to a normal working trot.

Never do this on the road, or on hard or slippery going. Furthermore at this stage the horse has not learnt the sideways driving aids, and in my opinion is not yet a safe ride on the roads.

Always make the young horse walk on up to the bit, and with a slight flexion to the right. This helps to keep him straight, and prevents him from shying into the road and becoming a hazard to traffic. Never slop along the road on a loose rein

PROGRESSIVE FLATWORK TRAINING

A few weeks will have been spent working in the school, interspersed with hacking out; as a result the horse has become fitter and should be ready to cope with more physically demanding work, namely a training programme of progressively more demanding schooling exercises. First of all he must be taught to move away from the leg, and this can be done by way of some simple school movements. I prefer to start with **shoulder-fore** in which the rider holds the

This horse is showing some strong, powerful, extended strides, but he is leaning on the rider's hand a little, so half halts will be necessary to teach him to have better self-carriage and to lighten his forehand more than is seen here. If the forehand is lighter his nose will be slightly in front of the vertical and the steps will be a little higher and longer

hindquarters on the track with the inside leg, feels the outside rein to bring the outside shoulder in from the track a little, and opens the inside hand to ask for a slight bend. This is the start of shoulder-in. I do this in walk, and then in trot and in canter, as it is a very good way to straighten your horse – his shoulders are narrower than his hips, so when riding in a straight line you are always having to keep the horse straight with your inside leg into your outside rein, which maintains a firmer contact in order to establish balance and maintain the speed. Once your horse answers your sideways pushing leg aids, these can be reinforced with a little tap with the whip behind the rider's leg if the horse does not respond sufficiently.

Another useful movement is the **turn on the forehand**, in which the horse is asked to move his hindquarters away from the leg. Properly executed, the hind legs describe a 180° half-circle, the outside hind leg stepping in front of the inside hind leg, with the forehand of the horse acting as pivot. To move his quarters to the left, feel the right rein so he turns head and neck slightly to the right, and apply the right leg one hand behind the girth; release your leg aid as soon as he responds to its sideways pressure: in this way he will learn that this is what you require of him, and your praise together with the repeating of the exercise a few times will soon make him responsive to your sideways leg aids. This movement will help you when riding out in the future, for example when you wish to open a gate: the horse must be responsive to your request to move up to and around the gate as you open it.

Leg-yielding is used to keep the horse between leg and hand, and to ask him to move forwards and sideways; it is a good suppling exercise as well as making him obedient. His body should be straight with a very slight flexion away from the movement; he moves on two tracks. Take care that he doesn't fall out through his shoulder; this is usually caused by too much bend away from the movement, which is incorrect. Starting in walk, the young horse soon learns to move away from the leg as he has been taught with shoulder-fore and turn on the forehand. To move him away from the left leg, apply the left leg one hand behind the girth, keeping the right leg just behind the girth as support and to ride him forward; his head should be flexed very slightly left, so the rider's left hand maintains a light contact, and the right controls the shoulders, maintains the balance and allows the flexion required in head and neck. Thus the rider must regulate the horse's forward and sideways steps with his seat, legs and hands to indicate to the horse where he is to go. For example, I begin by starting to ride down the centre line, then I push the horse forwards and sideways to the track, so he takes very shallow sideways steps with a very gradual angle, using the whole length of the school before reaching the outside track. Thus when turning down the centre line on the right rein, ride straight for two steps and then ask the horse to step away from the right leg towards the left-hand corner; this prevents him falling on the left shoulder. This procedure should be repeated on the other rein. When the horse accomplishes this easily in walk and on both reins, then practise the same movement in trot.

Shoulder-in is a more advanced version of shoulder-fore, with the horse moving on three tracks: inside foreleg, then outside foreleg on a parallel track with the inside hind leg, then outside hind leg. The horse should be about thirty degrees to the direction of the movement, and bent through his whole body away from the direction of the movement. This is a very useful exercise to make the horse supple through his body and rib-cage; it is a way of lightening the forehand and engaging the hindquarters because the inside hind leg has to push under the horse; and it is one of the most effective movements in straightening and balancing the horse. Start the movement in walk and take the shoulders in thirty degrees using the same aids as for shoulder-fore: inside leg into a firmer outside rein brings the shoulder in from the track, while the inside rein indicates a slight inside bend. The outside leg stops the quarters from escaping outwards.

Before asking for shoulder-in it is often helpful to ask for a ten-metre circle first, as this gives the horse the correct bend and helps to balance him. Shoulder-in can be used to help keep the horse straight, and is an excellent means of preventing him from shying or spooking at strange objects, especially when riding out on the roads, as his head is turned away from whatever it is that is likely to frighten him.

Increasing and decreasing the circle is a most effective exercise to supple the horse laterally: come from a twenty-metre circle down to a ten-metre circle, and after a couple of circles, ride in leg-yielding back to the twenty-metre circle. Changing the rein within a twenty-metre circle is also effective: ride one ten-metre half-circle with a change of direction to another ten-metre half-circle, taking up the new twenty-metre circle on the other rein. Make sure the horse stays in balance between both legs and both reins; if he falls

in with his shoulders he must be pushed out more strongly with the inside leg to make him stay in correct balance. It is this sort of repetition and dedication to detail in these early stages of training which will make the difference between the horse being responsive, obedient and balanced, and being on the forehand and slow to react to the rider's aids.

In the **half-pirouette** at walk, the horse moves his forehand in a large half-circle around his quarters which describe a smaller half-circle; the horse is bent in the direction in which he is moving. At this early stage this exercise constitutes the beginning of the half-pass. (Half-pass is not included here, as the horse must have much more collection than at this early stage in his training.) To teach the half-pirouette, I start by walking the horse in a half-circle, asking him to hold his quarters more steady and walk with slightly shorter steps sideways with the hind legs, while the forelegs make slightly larger steps. The inside leg on the girth keeps the horse going forwards, the outside leg applied one hand behind the girth stops the quarters moving outwards, while the outside rein controls the shoulders balancing the degree of the turn, and the inside rein indicates the direction and the bend. The seat and both legs are slightly forward-riding. The horse must not step backwards, and the sequence of four-time footfall must be clear and perfectly regular.

The **rein back** can be taught at this stage, though it should not be introduced too early – only when the horse understands the leg, seat and rein aids should you ask him to rein back with a rider. You have already introduced this movement to him when long-reining him, so he should understand the command 'back'.

The horse must be standing in a

balanced halt with a relaxed jaw and with his hind legs reasonably beneath him. The rider should then place both legs a bit further behind the girth, he should lighten the seat a little and push the horse forwards, but to a restraining rein: as the horse feels he cannot step forwards, so he will take a step back. Lighten the rein and leg aids as soon as he steps back; repeat these aids for each step until you wish to stop. When the horse understands the aids you will just have to lighten your seat and put both legs further behind the girth to make him step back until you ride him forwards again. To finish the movement and make the horse walk forwards again, move your legs into the normal forward riding position, and ride the horse forwards with a more upright seat.

The **serpentine** – three loops with a half-halt each time you cross the centre line – is another helpful balancing movement, and one that can be used to perfect the half-halt whenever a new movement has been taught such as leg-yielding or canter transitions. It is important to re-establish the early training of half-halt after the learning of new lessons so the horse does not become heavy in the rider's hand and muddled in his thoughts; it is also important to re-establish forward impulsion, for example by lengthening and shortening the steps. Once the three-loop serpentine has been established you can progress to four, five or six loops, though you would need a 20 x 60 metre arena.

The rider must always insist that the horse concentrates on his work when in trot and canter. If his mind is miles away, regain his attention by using exercises such as smaller circles, and transitions in quick succession from trot to walk, and trot to halt; and when he has been

Here Zebedee is shying at something to his left. Note how the rider is taking the right rein and using his right leg to stop the horse from falling in to the right, and running away from the problem. Allow the horse to accustom himself to any such 'frightener' by letting him keep his distance until he finds there is nothing to fear, and you can gradually take him nearer and nearer without any fuss. If this doesn't work, stop and let him look at and sniff the object until he is satisfied that there is nothing to be afraid of

concentrating well for a little while, then reward him with a little relaxation in walk on a long rein. All work and no rest makes all horses (and humans) dull and heavy!

When the horse is more established in his work it is important to be able to ride him away from the wall or track; a good start is to make **loops** in from the track of five to ten metres, both in trot and in canter so that the horse is learning to balance correctly between the seat, leg and the outside rein. First ride a trot circle in the corner of ten metres diameter, then ride the horse in from the track towards the centre marker X of the arena, and gradually ride a curve coming back out to the corner quarter marker. This is a very easy exercise in trot, but in canter it is more difficult for him as you will then be asking for the start of counter-canter. Therefore do it a few times on both reins in trot before you attempt it in canter, then the horse will understand the character of this new exercise before you strike off in canter. To start with you should only come a step or two in from the track; as the horse becomes better balanced then you can make the loop bigger and more to the centre line. When the horse is more advanced, at a much later stage in his training, this can be made into a three-loop serpentine, each loop going to the far side of the arena.

All these movements help the horse to become more supple, manoeuvrable and obedient to the leg aids; however, they must be used in a carefully structured way and must be introduced gradually over several weeks. It is through using all these simple school movements that the horse is kept interested and balanced, and can be taught the basics of transitions and half-halts within these movements.

TROTTING POLES

Trotting poles can be of great benefit in training, for all disciplines; they teach a horse to balance itself, to use its back and flex the joints, and to think for itself. Some horses get the idea of trotting poles very easily, and will walk over a pole on the ground straightaway; others make a huge fuss and are convinced the pole is going to eat them! The former type is easy, and will be happily trotting over poles on the first day. Start by walking over one pole, then over three placed 90cm (3ft) apart; when the horse is confident over these in walk, move them so they are 1.20m

(4ft) apart and trot over them. He must learn to take his time and to stay in rhythm, though it is up to the rider to regulate the pace and to place the horse correctly over the first pole. Always ride in rising trot to allow the horse plenty of freedom over his back, and so he can lower his head and look at what he is doing. He should approach on the bit, and through greater activity of the joints in his legs he will come a little more into the hand, which should be regulated accordingly; and when he is in balance the reins should be lightened to encourage him to take the rein and lower his head and use his back.

For short-striding horses it is

TURNING AWAY

With a horse that consistently tries to turn away from a pole on the ground, place a pole at right angles to a fence and put others to guide him in; keep your whip on the side away from the fence and give him a smart slap if he continues to be stupid about stepping over it. You must nevertheless give him time to think about what you are asking him to do. Sometimes it is helpful if an older horse gives him a lead, but he has obviously got to learn to do it by himself in time. With this type of horse it often pays to work him over poles every day for some days, until he comes to relax and accept what is being asked of him. Progress to different poles in different positions, and build up to three or five in a row placed so they can be taken on a circle, or when changing the rein across the diagonal, or perhaps down the centre line.

Start by introducing the youngster to a single pole on the ground

Asking Humbug to trot over it: he decides to jump it instead

sometimes a help to put the poles on a circle so they fan out from the centre, wider apart on the outside circumference, closer together on the inside. The inside ends of the poles can be raised to encourage a more collected trot, and the outside ends of the poles left on the ground for a more extended pace. Some horses take exception to walking over a pole on the ground, and even more to trotting poles, but you must be firm, and insist that the horse obeys your demands. In the first instant he will try to turn away from the pole, but you must not allow him to do this, and must turn him back the same way to face it. You must be resolute and make him wait, and look, and gradually insist that he walks over it; when he does go he may jump it awkwardly, in which case be sure you go 'with' him: do not get left behind the movement or catch him in the mouth. A

neck-strap is often a help when riding a horse which is silly about pole work, as you can hold it in one hand to help your balance, but it also allows your hand enough mobility to steer.

HACKING OUT

The young horse will have been hacking regularly round drives and tracks since he was broken in, but every horse needs variety and riding him in the open round a field would be a good change from your arena, as long as the ground conditions are reasonable. He should be taught to walk and later to trot round the field staying straight between both reins so that he moves in a straight line; if he is excited and not concentrating then take him on a circle or two, but as soon as possible continue on the straight. As you are

Trotting over it as he should, showing active use of his joints

Trotting over six poles, using head, neck and back which will help develop all the paces

riding the horse like this you must also teach him to move away from the leg – do not allow him to bulge his body and spook away from objects in the hedgerows. This is where shoulder-in and shoulder-fore can be used, to keep the horse straight and between both reins and thus prevent his shying. It is always a good idea to practise lateral work such as leg-yielding and shoulder-in in a field so that the horse is constantly responsive to your aids and learns to concentrate in all situations and surroundings. Some horses take time to settle and only quiet, sensible hacking with long spells of trotting – a couple of miles or more – will relax these hyperactive animals. Others take it all in their stride and don't need so much work.

Once the horse is obedient to these situations he should be ready to take on the road. If possible it is wise to go out initially with a couple of older horses as 'nannies', one in front and the other beside the young horse. Always remember to thank all drivers for slowing down, even if you didn't notice much change in speed! If they are given no thanks at all they will probably go even faster in the future.

Walking around the roads and giving the horse time to see different objects is important. When you move into trot make it slow and rhythmical without too much impulsion as it is easy for a horse to slip on the tarmac. When riding past anything strange or potentially alarming, keep his head turned away from the object by using your right leg and right rein, keeping him balanced in your left rein (assuming you are riding on the left side of the road; if on the right, reverse your aids); these are the aids for shoulder-in, and will help you to keep the horse straight at all times.

Humbug hacking out. Developing the trot on uphill inclines helps to build up the horse's muscle over his back, loins and quarters

Uphill work also increases the activity in the hind legs and helps teach the horse to maintain his balance within a pace

The horse should be made to walk on in a correct outline and up to the bridle, using the muscles of the neck and back, and making his hindquarters work in pushing the stride forwards with the shoulders swinging and loose. The trot should be slow and rhythmical, again with the horse working through his whole body. In this way you will build up the muscle structure. Trotting uphill will also improve the heart and lung capacity, and he will really have to use his hind legs to push himself up the incline.

THE PHYSICAL BENEFITS OF ROADWORK

Walking and slow trotting on a hard road surface is the traditional and proven way of tightening up a horse's legs, bones, muscles, ligaments and tendons, but it must be conducted in moderation and sensibly. A spanking extended trot on a flapping rein is of no benefit at all, and could very easily end up with the horse slipping or falling over; besides, it will jar his legs and feet and make him more susceptible to navicular disease, pedalostitis and damaged joints.

TYPICAL EVASIONS

Napping

Some horses will try and whip round when they see something they dislike or don't want to pass; however, they must not be allowed to turn round as this is the start of napping, and if once they are allowed to get away with it, it will continue. Always correct the horse by turning him back the way he has come – do not allow him to make a circle; it may take you more time and considerable argument, but he *must* do as he is told. If he whips round to the left, then you must stop him quickly with the right rein and put your stick in the left hand to reinforce your rein aid and leg; he may need a sharp smack, too, to make him understand that this behaviour is not acceptable. As soon as he moves in the required direction, reward him. Some riders *ask* for young horses to nap because they ride them absentmindedly in a strange area on a totally loose rein, quite unaware themselves of anything that is going on around them or likely to spook or frighten the horse. This is not the way a young horse should be ridden: you should not take your mind off the horse for one second, you must be alert yourself, and you should anticipate what a horse may be frightened of before it happens – only then can you hope to keep him straight, and reassure him so that he is prevented from whipping round before it ever happens.

Some years ago we were sent a four-year-old mare, Wellingtonia, to sort out because when her elderly owner got on her for a ride she would not go more than a hundred yards from home; the mare obviously considered this was quite far enough to have to go, so she would stand on her hind legs and return to her stable. Soon she refused even to leave the yard, which is when we got her! After a little sorting out with a sharp rider who knew the problem, and with the assistance of a lunge whip, she was soon going forwards and doing as she was told. She was given lots of obedience work in the school and

showed a good aptitude for jumping; after a couple of weeks' schooling she was going very well, and was returned to her owner.

A month later she was back again with the same problem – the rides had gradually got shorter and shorter until once again they only got to the yard gate! With positive riding she was again instantly sorted out – a good kick and a pat – and was also sent hunting with my daughter to give her more forward ideas. She became a very good hunter, and her owner decided to sell her, having decided they were obviously not suited to each other. Several people came to try her and thought her lovely in the confines of the arena and when jumping in the field; they all then asked if they could take her down the road, which we thought would be fine, but each time she returned sooner than the prospective buyer anticipated – she could feel they were not really positive riders and immediately picked up her old habits. I despaired of ever selling this mare, and finally a client of ours kindly bought her for my daughter to ride. In fact she went on to compete in the European Junior 3DE Championships in Rome, also at Wembley in the Horse of the Year Show, and then became a schoolmistress training students to Advanced Medium level; but until the day she retired to be a broodmare she would still turn round and come home if given the chance!

Bolting
Many young horses will occasionally take off in frightened reaction to some object or occurrence, and this situation can be readily exacerbated by a rider panicking because the horse is going faster than he intended. A horse can also become naughty from over-freshness, and in

this case may shoot off at the slightest provocation unnecessarily: this must be stopped in the early stages. First, bring him back under control: keep your hands down near to the wither, shorten your left rein and put your fist on the neck just in front of the wither as a brace, and gradually stop the horse with the other rein, your legs and your voice. If he has been naughty I would turn him in a small circle on both reins and then make him stop again; then work him hard in the same area from where he galloped off, in smaller circles on both reins until he is quieter, relaxed and moving forward on bigger circles with a relaxed neck. He must be made to do lots of downward transitions to halt, and up to trot and back to halt again, with the rider using all the halt and half-halt aids that he has been taught previously. Only put the horse away when he has worked well and is obedient.

It would also be advisable perhaps to reduce the protein content of his feed, and possibly to turn him out in the field to let off any excess energy which may be the cause of his silliness.

If a horse bolts with his head right up you must try not to panic, but wait for the head to come down – you could also lower your hands so that the bit is working on the bars of the mouth and not on the molars, when he will have no feeling and will not respond to your restraining aids. Only when the initial fright has passed can you start to slow the horse down, but you must try not to panic yourself as this will make the horse more nervous. Stop the horse in the same way, but reassure him when you have come to a halt, and calm him down by walking quietly in a circle until you have control of the situation.

Running Back
This is a nasty habit and must be corrected as soon as possible. First, avoid causing the horse to panic by kicking furiously with the legs or using the whip madly, as this tends to make him go back even faster. I have found that it is often better to sit still and wait for the horse to settle and think a bit; only when he seems to be more settled mentally would I ask him to move forwards again. I also find it more beneficial to turn the horse in tiny circles several times, first one way and then the other, so that he is a bit disorientated; then he is more likely to listen. If, once he has had a chance to take stock of the situation, he still tries to run back then I would have to resort to one or two sharp smacks with the whip and may even need an assistant to get behind with a lunge whip to help send him forwards. The rider must be sure to go 'with' the horse when he does move forwards again – if you get left behind and catch him in the mouth you will be punishing him for doing what you want him to do. Obviously you must then reward him for doing as you ask, and relax him. This is just what Wellingtonia used to do, though she used to rear up as well! We did have to have quite a fit assistant for a few sessions, but as I have described, with a positive rider she soon settled down and became a very good mare.

Rearing
This is usually associated with napping or whipping round on the hind legs away from some object. Often a horse will try not to turn back the way he swung out, and will jump up and down threatening to rear. If a horse does stand up, try to make it fairly unpleasant for him, either by keeping hold of the reins, or by riding him forwards firmly

with a smart smack with the whip. If he stands up I shake the bit in his mouth until he comes down, and then give him time to think about the situation; often this is enough. My logic is to make it extremely unpleasant for the horse when he is standing on his hind legs, and very pleasant when he is being good, so that he soon realises which is right and which is wrong. Many people will release all contact with the horse's mouth as soon as it rears, so it very soon finds out that this is an easy evasion, instead of it being the exact opposite. There *are* times, however, when you have to release the contact for your own safety.

Bucking

This can be caused by fright; therefore try and sit quietly! Attempt to stop the bucking by trying to keep the horse's head up – raise your hands and talk to the horse, saying 'Woah', or 'Steady'. Then reassure him and walk quietly until he is relaxed. Be sure you try to stay calm yourself, and be quick to try and stop the same thing happening again.

If the horse is persistently naughty then cut down his hard feed and possibly turn him out all night before you ride him. If he continues to think about bucking then ride him more forwards, keeping his head up and driving him forwards more and more until he gives up. I would work him well and give him plenty to occupy his mind. Also be aware that the saddle could be pinching him, and that he is bucking because he is uncomfortable. Consider therefore changing to a better fitting saddle. However, I have had this particular problem happen several times, and usually it is because the horse is too fresh – that is over-fed and under-worked!

CORRECTIVE MEASURES

If you have a horse who insists on bucking without any obvious reason, try riding him in a cherry roller gag snaffle. The horse is respectful of this bit and cannot get his head down as easily as with an ordinary snaffle, so you can concentrate on riding him forward and up to the contact. Another method is to ride in a ploughed field where the going is deep; the horse has to behave or he could easily lose his footing. Take care not to overdo this as he could easily pull a tendon or overreach.

RIDING OVER DIFFERENT TERRAIN

It is important to teach the horse to carry himself over different terrain, and especially so for the potential event horse. He has to learn to trot and later to canter over ridge and furrow, to stay balanced up and down steep inclines, and to go through mud and softer going. Trotting over heather is very good for making the horse use his limbs, as the coarse plant tickles his fetlocks and makes him pick his legs up as if he were trotting over poles on the ground.

At this early stage it is also important that a horse learns to trust his rider implicitly, even when it is not obvious as to where he is going, for example from a field into a dark wooded area. With cross-country jumping in mind, many a refusal has been caused by a rider not appreciating the effect darkness has on a horse's mind. However, he must get used to continuing to go forwards, even when he cannot see a way out. Keep the horse up to the bit with your legs, and slightly bend him in the direction you are going to take so that he gets used to the directional aid – all part of the process of him learning to trust you.

Muddy areas can cause some

horses a great deal of concern, but again, a horse must trust his rider that such areas are safe to go through – just be quite sure that the one you are trying to negotiate isn't a very deep clay-hole! Thus find a dark, muddy patch that isn't deep, and treat the situation as you would when you teach a horse to walk through water: take your time, and after he has had a good look and a sniff if he wants to, persuade him to go forwards. Give him a lead with an older horse, and walk him through the mud until he is confident and not rushing through it. It is only when he relaxes that he will learn to gain confidence in you as a rider, and to go where you ask him.

Learning about Water

In the first instance it is imperative to find a safe and easy access to calm water, *not* a steep and slippery bank into a fast-flowing river. A shallow lake or overflow from a river is ideal to start with, and as the water is usually clear the horse can see the bottom. Let the horse lower his head and look at the water – all horses like to sniff it out and this often gives them confidence. In no way hurry a horse as this will fluster him and he will be more likely to try and turn away; keep your leg on him and keep him straight. The older horse can give him a lead and paddle about until the youngster takes the initiative to go in himself; and it often gives a horse confidence to see a person walk in and out of the water, particularly if the person then comes up to the horse and talks to him quietly. Beware when your horse first gets his feet wet as he may go in with a leap, and could jump into you or your schoolmaster.

When finally he does get into the water, let him walk about in it and get used to it; let him eat some grass

from the side and enjoy it – though do beware, as some horses will paw and enjoy it so much that they may try to lie down and roll! Once the horse is confident in the water, move him out and in as often as you like, so he continues to enjoy it. When you bring the horse out of the water the first time you may find it a little difficult to get him back in again; but the time taken at this initial

stage is extremely important in gaining the horse's obedience and establishing his confidence in the rider.

Next, take him to some other water; a clear river is very good as it is always changing in appearance. Use the same quiet insistence until the horse is confident. I do feel that a lot of people get into trouble by asking a horse such a big question as

going into water too soon in his training, before he is fully obedient to the leg and rein aids. If he is very green and obviously unsure of what you are asking him to do, you are more likely to end up punishing him by trying to keep him straight, as he does not understand the aids well enough to be obedient to what you are asking him.

Catherston Zebedee's first

Dance in the Dark has to go in and out of the water several times to try and persuade Zebedee to come a little nearer

introduction to water was far quicker than I had anticipated! He had always been a somewhat nervous horse, but obedient when asked to go forwards, and had experience jumping clear round jumping, small grids and doubles; I therefore felt it was time to ask him a more demanding question. We went down to the river with Catherston Dance in the Dark who had already been introduced to it – needless to say, he took it on with only a casual glance, and enjoyed splashing about on this his initial visit as the 'older and wiser escort'. So we arrived at the river, and Dance in the Dark strolled in happily as usual while Zebedee shivered with fright about four metres from the water's edge, snorting. James sat quietly on him and reassured him with a stroke on the neck while I – being brave on my feet! – walked into the water and out again and went to talk to him.

In the meantime Lizzie on Dance in the Dark had come out of the river towards us, making Zebedee

Introducing Zebedee to water: at first he was reluctant to come anywhere near the water at all, so I go in, walking quietly so as not to splash, to reassure him that it is safe

cringe with even more fright when he saw the splashes from the other horse's hooves. So we sent Lizzie back into the river and out the other side to encourage Zebedee at least to get himself nearer to his problem! James gradually asked Zebedee to walk forwards nearer the river. I noticed how nervous he was of the splash from the water, so walked in and out making as little splash as possible with my feet, then going up to Zebedee to reassure him. He gradually lowered his head and

looked at the water as he got closer. I gave him a little grass, which he thought was a wonderful idea and proceeded to graze by the river's edge which gave him a lot of confidence among his snorts.

After a few minutes James took up the reins and asked him to move forwards into the water. A bit more dithering, and then in true *Magic Roundabout* style, Zebedee bounced – 'boing, boing, boing' – into, through and out of the river with more splashes over me than water left in it! He was rewarded and made a fuss of. However, he was now on the opposite bank and had to come back to get home. Lizzie gave him another lead, and after further dithering he leapt again into the river; but James managed to make him stop this time halfway across, patting him and letting him sniff the water, which he did with horror. After a lot of reassuring Lizzie joined him, and they both walked about in the river until Zebedee was calm and relaxed. Then they both came out, and James took Zebedee back into the water by himself where he made a real fuss of him. They then proceeded happily home, having accomplished a successful training session.

Catherston Humbug's reaction to walking into water was totally different, other than being initially

A POSITIVE APPROACH

Remember that a calm, firm approach is essential when introducing a horse to anything new. If you are not positive and committed then he will be nervous. That is why many good horses will refuse to jump an obstacle with a faint-hearted rider because they pick up on the jockey's state of mind and respond accordingly. Change the rider and the same horse will immediately become a positive jumper, so long as the rider is riding forwards strongly to the other side of the fence.

After some time Zebedee launches himself off the bank, and plunges straight across to the other side in three great leaps!

terrified at the thought – also by three ducks that decided to leave the area on our approach, causing both Lizzie and me to be nearly deposited on the ground as the horses whipped round at lightning speed! Confidence regained and riders restored to the correct position in the saddle, we approached the river again. Lizzie on Catherston Dance in the Dark went into the river and out the other side; Humbug was horrified, and plainly demonstrated

that he had no intention of following and getting his feet wet. With gentle persuasion he got closer to the water, but insisted on rearing up and trying to depart towards home. He got a sharp smack for this evasion, and also a firm rein when he was on his hind legs which made it rather unpleasant for him. He soon realised it wasn't getting him anywhere, so he stopped and looked at the water, eating grass from the bank and gradually working his way

All in all I was pleased that Humbug had put his trust in me so quickly, even though he had started by being naughty, and that he had so soon changed his mind and became a biddable ride.

Always be aware that when one horse follows another into the water, the horse behind may cause the water to splash the horse in front, so allow plenty of room before following another horse into water. Similarly the rider in front should be aware that he could be splashed, and must be ready not to get 'left behind' and catch his horse in the teeth if it jumps forwards suddenly. Plenty of time must be taken in order to build up a young horse's

On his second attempt James manages to stop him halfway: he reassures him, and lets him sniff the water and paddle about

closer to the water's edge.

Once he had sniffed the water he seemed to get his confidence, and one step at a time walked very slowly into the river. Initially he was quite nervous about getting his legs wet, but he soon overcame this and walked backwards and forwards through it in a much shorter time than I had anticipated. I made him turn away from the other horse and from home and go by himself into the water, which he did very well.

confidence about going in and out of water until he is really enjoying it; let him graze on the bank while standing in the water, and generally splash about. Choose a hot day when he will like cooling off. Take him back to the same place several times so that he is happy about entering the water in familiar surroundings; then take him to water in a different surrounding so that he learns to enter water anywhere, confidently.

By now you and your horse can go almost anywhere. This initial period of riding and training is crucial to the partnership of trust between horse and rider that you should be hoping to achieve. Once you have laid a solid foundation of confidence, you must seriously consider getting him fitter and more muscled up in order to start more serious schooling, and training him to jump.

Zebedee and Dance in the Dark walk quietly and much more confidently up and down the river

Early Jumping and Fitness Work

It is very important that the young horse is fittened gradually, both physically and mentally, for the job you are asking him to do; this can take a few months or even longer depending on the horse's initial muscle tone – some horses are naturally more muscled up than others, and these are quicker to train as they are stronger over their back already and better suited to carrying the weight of a rider. A skinny, upside-down-looking horse will take a great deal of time and correct feeding to build up in order to be strong enough to take on a career, be it eventing, dressage or jumping; it can take as much as six months longer, and it is imperative to realise that you cannot hurry this process. Both types of horse can be equally successful if correctly trained, and if the rider has the patience to wait. Every horse is an individual and should be treated as such, and this concerns his mental attitude just as much as his physical ability.

Fitness is vital for any horse: his legs, feet and joints are perhaps the most important parts, as without a sound horse you have nothing, and an unfit horse is far more likely to strain a ligament or pull a tendon than a horse which is correctly trained and prepared physically for the occasion. You must build up to maximum fitness gradually by following a carefully structured programme (see pages 150–4).

I consider it important that every horse is able to expand his lungs well, whether he is a showjumper, an eventer or a dressage horse, therefore faster work to some degree should always be included in a training programme. At the top level in all these disciplines the horses have to be really fit so that they do not tire at the end of the course or test; if they do, it will not help their performance, and moreover is bad for their mental attitude – when asked to compete in the future, they will very probably remember the fatigue they experienced on their previous outing and be less than enthusiastic to work with you on the next occasion.

BUILDING UP PHYSICAL FITNESS

Your young horse is already working on the roads and trotting and cantering up hills, and you should concentrate on continuing this work on a daily basis to build up his muscles and tighten the tendons. He will be reasonably fit already as a result of lungeing and being broken in, so the fittening requirement will not be the same as when bringing a horse up from grass and having to do four weeks' walking exercise. However, it is sensible to make a progressive plan both for his fittening and for his training so that you do three days' fittening interspersed with three days' training each week, with one day off when he can relax in the field for exercise and a change. Increase the time or the distance which you work each day and adjust his feeding according to the amount of work, and to suit his temperament and condition.

Thus a four-year-old should have at least an hour's work a day if hacking out, which may include hill work. It is always preferable to hack him out at walk for twenty minutes before starting his school work, as this helps to loosen his muscles and frame and means he is doing something interesting before the schooling session. About thirty to forty minutes' work is sufficient if he is being schooled or having jumping training. After you have finished schooling it is beneficial to walk the horse for ten to fifteen minutes to cool him down and let his muscles relax before taking him to the stables. If he has sweated up then wash him off with a warm saline solution, making sure that you wash well round the elbows and girth area and all over the horse's back where the saddle has been; this should help prevent girth galls and saddle sores. If he has sweated up over his loins and quarters this area should be washed off as well to prevent him breaking out in a cold sweat. The excess water should be taken off with a scraper and the horse rugged up immediately with a sweat rug and cooler or a towelling sheet, depending on the weather.

The legs should be hosed to cool down the circulation, and then dried with a towel. If you are hosing down a horse's legs in the winter months, be sure that you put on an extra rug to keep the horse warm as hosing his legs will also cool his whole body temperature considerably – there are many blood vessels in the legs which are close to the skin. Always dry his heels well with a towel to prevent cracked heels, and keep a close eye on his legs for injury. If he has had a strong work-out, such as cross-country schooling or hill work with a canter, it might be a good idea to put dry bandages on him to help keep his legs warm and give them a little support.

Coping with Different Temperaments

Working up and down hills is one of the best ways to get a horse fit, and particularly of making a lazy horse use himself. With a lazy horse it is helpful to have another horse trotting alongside to encourage it and make it feel more competitive; this type is also helped by cantering it alongside another horse and asking it to increase and decrease the speed, which should make it a little more excited and more forward-thinking. It is always a good idea to let the lazy horse get his head well in front of his companion before you pull up and walk home. One of our horses, Xenarchus, was very lazy until he found out about galloping and decided he really liked it; and although he ended up a dressage horse, he only performed to his best if he was galloped about behind the lorries, trucks and vans and then taken straight into the arena. He was given a great deal of fast work training, and then began really to like competition.

With an excitable animal, on the other hand, it is not advisable to have a horse alongside, as the hot sort naturally likes to be in front – competition will make him want to rush on and he will learn to take hold of the bit too strongly. For this type of horse a lot of patience and quiet trotting alone is much more beneficial. You must teach him, by repeated half-halts, to trot at the speed required, and encourage him to relax so that he is trotting with his head in an easy, low position, taking the rein correctly. Once he is settled in trot you can increase and decrease the pace a little bit, but don't do anything dramatic as this will only excite him. The same work must be achieved in canter so he learns to lengthen and shorten the steps. Now and again he should be allowed to stretch out and gallop on, but when cantering he must never get beyond half speed; though he should be given enough freedom to learn that what you want is for him to stay in a relaxed frame and to respond to your downward aids readily and easily. Thus when he is travelling at a reasonable speed and seems settled in his work, it is important that the rider tries to relax his hands so the horse understands he is at the required speed – the rider must try not to be constantly restraining him, or he will actually encourage the horse to take too strong a hold; it takes two to pull! The rider must also be careful to steady a horse from a half-speed canter slowly, and not expect it to come back to a collected canter in a few strides by pulling roughly on the reins or by turning in sharp circles, as this will unbalance him and could cause him to pull a tendon. Another of our horses, Desert Storm, the granddam of Catherston Dance in the Dark, was very excitable and would *never* settle behind another horse, and would never walk home. I tried every possible method but we both only got more upset, so I decided there and then that we would trot until it became unwise because of the downhill slope, and then I would dismount and lead the mare home rather than arriving back hot and sweaty. Luckily her grandson is happy to go first or last!

Jetstream, showing excellent technique in her early jumping

EARLY JUMPING LESSONS

I feel that it is advantageous for all horses to learn to jump, including dressage horses: jumping provides a refreshing change in their training routine and helps to make them think for themselves, as well as use their backs and open their shoulders. Some horses may not be particularly gifted at jumping, but my top horses – Xenocles, Dutch Courage, Dutch Gold, Catherston Dutch Bid and Catherston Dazzler – have all enjoyed and benefited from jumping in the course of their careers, whether it was showjumping, working hunter classes or eventing. Dutch Gold and Catherston Dazzler in particular have been capable of taking time off from an international dressage competition to go to the showjumping collecting ring in order to pop over the international jumpers' practice fence, and they have both competed successfully in jumping and eventing; given the opportunity and the rider, both would have excelled in any of the three disciplines.

JUMPING DISTANCES
Distances – A placing pole before a fence can vary from 2.50m to 2.80m depending on the size of the fence and how close you wish the horse to come to the fence.
Jumping distances from trot for one stride – 6.00m to 6.25m – as the fences build up distance can lengthen if necessary 6.25m to 7.00m. For two strides from trot 9.10m to 9.70m.
When jumping from canter – Lengthen distances to 6.50m to 7.50m for one stride or 10.00m to 10.60m for two strides. These can also be varied for shortening the horse or for making him go more forward by lengthening the stride up to 11.00m, or 10.80m maximum when jumping a big vertical. If the horse is gaining too much speed, shorten the distances.

I would suggest that a cross-pole, generally with a placing pole 2.5m (9ft 3in) in front of it, is a good obstacle for a young horse carrying a rider to start off with, particularly as most youngsters will have had jumping practice on the lunge or when being loose schooled. Ride him in trot, and give him a few jumps over the same obstacle; change it to a vertical rail, and then introduce a parallel rail. When the horse is confidently jumping this small fence you can put a placing plank on the ground on the landing side; this makes the horse use his head, neck and back while jumping and helps him to land in balance. When jumping young horses, place the fences so that sometimes a fence can act as a wing on one side to help keep the horse straight; though basically he must be kept straight

Jetstream, again showing very good style. Take care that a horse like this does not overjump and frighten itself

Zebedee not sure about fillers: they are pulled apart to start with, then pulled in together beneath the pole as he gains in confidence

Zebedee very shortly afterwards jumping the wall and parallel with great confidence and style

between the reins by sympathetic but positive forward riding with the leg aids.

Gradually introduce different fillers to the fences so that the young horse learns to accept all sorts of different colours and shapes; this keeps his interest and tests his courage. He can now learn to jump small courses and related distances. In his approach to a fence he must learn to keep straight, and to continue after it in a balanced manner so that he can approach the next fence correctly between hand and leg. When you first introduce your horse to jumping a course start with no more than four fences so that the horse has to concentrate on just a few different things and only for a short space of time – if you tackle a complete course straight off he is bound to get tired, both physically and mentally, and probably faster and faster as he gradually loses balance and then control.

With a very free-going horse it is often a good idea to jump a fence and then halt and reward him, and only then repeat the exercise. Soon the horse will anticipate the halting after the fence and will want to stop for himself, putting you in a much better position to ride him to the next fence as he will not be running into your hand but waiting and listening for your commands. Another way is to put placing planks on both sides of the fence: jump it one way, halt at a reasonable distance after the fence, then turn the horse round and quietly allow him to walk towards the fence again; allow him to trot just before the placing plank, and jump the fence by closing your lower leg gently round him on the approach so that he knows what you are asking of him.

Gridwork
Any sort of gridwork is excellent for developing the horse's gymnastic ability, teaching him to use his head, to jump in a balanced manner and with a good bascule, and to learn to adjust his stride. Generally I start by

(Left and below) Humbug jumping a grid which has been built up to a bounce of cross-poles, then one stride to a parallel

jumping a double of small fences with one stride in between; the horse can see clearly what he has to do, and he knows there is room for him to land and continue over the second obstacle. Start with a small double, the two fences being 5.5 – 6m (16 – 18ft) apart; vertical obstacles are the easiest to start with, then progress to making the second obstacle a parallel. Approach in trot. Soon you can make a two-stride double with the fences 10 – 11m (30 – 33ft) apart.

Once the horse is confidently jumping doubles of one and two

(Above and right) A more advanced grid: Dance in the Dark working through a sequence of three cross-poles at bounce distance to a one-stride vertical

strides then these can be built up gradually into a more demanding grid; start with a bounce followed by one stride to a parallel, for example. Take care not to build up too much for the horse to take in, as this could upset his confidence. Start with a placing pole, a small vertical 2.5m (9ft 3in) away, another vertical 3 metres (10ft) away, then one 5.5 – 6m (16 – 18ft) stride to a parallel; later you might add another parallel

or vertical at 10 – 11m (30 – 33ft), or two strides away. Distances very much depend on the horse and his attitude to jumping: if he is not very forward-going for example, then make him go more forwards by making the distances gradually longer; if he is too keen, then keep them shorter, as this will make a horse shorten himself and be quicker in lifting the forearms, and he learns not to rush at the fences, provided the rider does not interfere. The rider must try not to shorten the horse while jumping, but should just keep him in balance and let the distances themselves slow him. Putting a parallel at the end of a grid encourages a horse to use himself and bascule well.

When the horse is confident and reasonably fit, a grid can be built up to three bounce fences to make the horse more athletic with his front legs and to build up his back muscles and the muscles over the quarters. These bounce fences can be

BENEFITS

Gridwork training also teaches the rider to be supple and athletic, to trust the horse, and to learn not to interfere with him by pulling on the reins. It is excellent for teaching the rider to balance and keep his position over a fence, with the lower leg firm in its position and the upper body supple and in balance over the fence. The hands and arms must not be fixed on the neck, but should be free and supple, and follow the movement of the horse's head and allow him to take the rein as and when he needs it.

followed by a one-stride to a two-stride distance, and back to a one-stride for the more advanced horse. You must obviously work up gradually to this, and must assess your horse's technique, fitness and ability before asking such an advanced question. None of these fences needs to be excessively high; in fact more is gained by jumping smaller, wider fences with varying distances as this improves his technique and physique.

Rushing a Fence

Pulling on the reins when the horse is jumping a grid, and particularly when he is rushing a fence, will only make him more nervous and cause him to rush more. With a horse that does rush and get worried, try the following: stop him near the fence, make him do a few backward steps, then ask him to pop over the fence quietly on a loose rein from your rein back. Don't hurry him; he can easily jump a metre (3ft) from a walk. If he changes his rhythm when approaching an obstacle and raises his head, he is obviously feeling a bit anxious so allow him to jump, then come again. He may tense up again when you start to approach the jump, in which case do a circle in front of the fence, in control, until you feel him relax – then approach the fence again. Don't give him too much time to see the fence. It is often a help with this type to keep coming on a circle, so position two or three jumps in different places so you can single out one on one circle, then jump a different one on the next circle so that he doesn't know which you are going to do. Don't go on too long without a rest period, and keep changing the rein.

Refusing

First find out why the horse refused. Is he frightened of the look of the

jump? In this case show him the obstacle and reassure him that it won't hurt him, unless he hits it! Remember to sit in a relaxed manner when he does stand and sniff at the fence, as your relaxation will give him confidence.

Are you, as rider, being positive when you ask the horse to jump the fence, or are you chickening out yourself, either miles away or at the last minute because you are nervous and not really confident about jumping? More horses are spoilt by nervous riders, who are really not aware that it is *they* who are the problem, but who then blame the horse. This situation is often made glaringly evident when a more experienced and confident rider gets on the same horse and it immediately finds its confidence and jumps superbly.

Some people find confidence in a certain type of horse and ride it well and with great success, but meet with disaster on one of different type or temperament. Some riders who have had a fall are inclined to lose confidence, and simply do not indicate to the horse any really positive intention, perhaps due to their fear of falling again; thus their riding as they come in to a fence is hesitant and passive, with the result that the horse comes in on a shortening stride and little impulsion and therefore gets under the fence for take-off. These riders need to get back to riding forwards and positively over fences as soon as possible so they regain their eye for a fence and restore a good active rhythm; otherwise they seriously risk falling again due to lack of impulsion.

Did the horse get punished when he last jumped a fence by being jabbed in the mouth by your loss of balance? This is a fault which I see most riders failing to put right – but no one is perfect and we have all been left behind, unintentionally punishing the horse when we really didn't mean to. Besides, young horses can jump very awkwardly, and it is very difficult to be 'with' them all the time; it is a good idea to have a neck-strap with a young horse as he will rather leap *at* the fences, and then there is something to hold on to, if necessary, rather than just the reins. In this case, where bad riding has caused the horse to refuse, we have to set about restoring his confidence carefully: lower the jump, slow the pace, then with firm legs and positive riding ask the horse to jump the fence again. If he still refuses, lower the jump more, even to poles on the ground; but then insist he jumps it, even if you have to use the whip to get what you want. Of course, as soon as he does jump the poles, reward him and do them again until he is jumping without you having to push him. Then you can gradually increase the size again, and all should be well.

Some young horses refuse the first time they approach any new obstacle. These must be very firmly ridden and kept busy, as they will probably try every sort of evasion – whipping round, leaping to the side, running back, rearing and so on. They need a good rider who can cope with every situation so that they realise that such antics are not going to disturb the rider, and that they are going to have to do as they are told eventually. Keep the fences low, and put up plenty of them in different places. Remember, trot is a good pace for a young horse to jump from, as its two-time stride brings him nearer to the fence for take-off. Canter is a three-beat stride and is therefore longer, and so the horse is more inclined to jump flat and lose his technique. Galloping

RUNNING OUT

Running out to one or other side of a fence must be quickly rectified. Try not to let the horse get past the wing, stop him, and turn him back the way he tried to run out so that he finds escape difficult. If he has run out to the left side of the fence, stop him quickly and turn him back to the right, then re-approach the fence with your whip in the left hand. When he has learnt that it is much easier and more comfortable to jump the fence, then he will cease running out.

about over fences achieves nothing in teaching a young horse to jump.

There are other things you must think about if a horse suddenly refuses to jump: do his feet hurt? Is he moving freely and sound? Is he ill? Does his back hurt? Any of these ailments will make a horse unwilling to jump – or even work at all! – and you should call in your vet if you consider he has a physical problem.

Improving Technique

When he has learnt to trot over jumps in different parts of the arena, teach him to canter slowly over the fences in the same way that you trotted over them, in a good, balanced canter, taking a fence whenever you feel he is happy and confident. I wouldn't keep the fences too small now or he could become careless. Keep him interested by using different fillers, and start to use related distances between the fences so that you can move steadily from one fence to another in a forward and balanced canter.

Unfortunately not every rider has an eye for a stride when approaching an obstacle. This is why it is so important to school the horse until he has a balanced canter which you can regulate to be a little more forward or a little more collected; then if you find you are on a poor stride, you can either collect the

Humbug was jumping rather flat, so to get him to use himself better he is asked to jump a square oxer; however, he loses confidence and runs out (he would be brought back to halt immediately and taken back)

The front rail of the oxer is lowered, and on his second attempt he learns to do it correctly

horse a little more or lengthen the stride slightly into the fence to make his take-off easier and in balance. The horse also has to learn to look after *himself*, and when jumping over small fences as a novice you should not interfere too much with his stride, other than to keep him balanced and in a rhythm: he should learn to shorten and lengthen his stride himself by eyeing up the fence and using his brain to assess his take-off. If you do all the work at this stage, you will have to continue doing all the work when the fences get bigger, and the horse will learn to become lazy, with no instinct for self-preservation.

At a later stage in training you should teach the horse to alter his pace between fences with greater responsiveness – for example, ask him to take one less stride in your related distance; another time ask him to jump more slowly and put in one extra stride – 'compress' him with your leg into your hand, and keep your body upright while you are steadying him. These are useful exercises to make the horse listen to the rider, and they also help you to keep a rhythm, which is important in any high-class performance.

MORE ADVANCED SCHOOLING

Your horse is by now used to being ridden on roads and tracks and in the open over fields; at this stage in his training he should be listening to you more, and you can take advantage of the natural terrain for a variety of fittening and schooling work. For example, use upward inclines to trot the horse up, to increase his muscle tone and to build him up before asking him to do more complicated work. Teach him to respond to the aids when riding uphill and downhill; he must learn to balance himself on the downward slopes, and not run away with the force of gravity, so transitions through half-halts on the downward slopes are very important; even when making the horse come from trot to halt he must learn to be responsive and obedient. When halting, let him stand and relax until asked to go forwards again. Uphill inclines can help improve the impulsion in the trot, and the length of stride. It is important with the young horse to encourage him to trot with more power up the hills, thus improving his impulsion for his extended paces. Some horses extend the paces easily, and others are inclined to run. This is where hill work is helpful as they have to push from behind, and must lift and lighten the shoulders or they will fall over. The horse must be ridden up to the rein, and should maintain the correct outline when going up and down hills.

Do not expect the horse to produce too many extended steps for too long. It is better to do a few steps in a more collected pace and then go forwards again several times so that the horse can balance in between the spells of lengthened stride, rather than doing a long distance of extended steps: this would probably end up very unbalanced and messy, just a long line of horse running fast into your hands. This is of no benefit at all. When the horse is stronger and older then you can ask for longer periods of power.

The same control must be displayed in canter, when you should be able to control the speed on the downward slopes, as well as allowing the horse to lengthen his stride on the upward slopes. The rider should always be able to collect and shorten the steps whenever he wishes.

Training for Jumping and Cross-Country

At this stage the young horse's education is progressing well: he is learning about general sights and sounds when he goes out hacking and he is reasonably fit; he should be going in a round novice outline, and be obedient and confident when asked to jump small courses and any natural hazard you might meet when out on a hack. It is time therefore to give him more to think about, and to train him to tackle more natural obstacles such as he might find in a cross-country course. You don't want to be on your dressage horse at a show and find that you cannot get to where you want to go because he won't go over a ditch, for example.

EXPERIENCE AND TECHNIQUE

All young horses should be given the schooling so as to gain experience in cross-country jumping and showjumping before you even

Dance in the Dark jumping a log pile confidently and with ease

*Humbug jumping his first
log with a small drop landing*

consider taking them to any competitions. There are many courses available for hire, with good going and a variety of small fences and combinations of all types. It is advisable to take a 'schoolmaster' with your youngster to give him a lead if necessary over the most spooky ditches, banks and so on. Study the course; once you have warmed up over a few of the more straightforward fences, show him some of the more difficult ones – let him tackle these individually so he can gain confidence, then later you can ride between five and eight fences at a good forward canter so he realises there is always more to come after each fence, and learns to move from one to another with purpose and enthusiasm.

How many schooling sessions you will have to do before you take your young horse to his first competition will depend on his temperament, fitness and ability. Before he competes it is advisable to take the horse to the same course on another day, and start him much as you would for a competition, jumping a course of between ten and fifteen fences straight off, starting with some easy fences to get him going forwards and up to the bridle before tackling any question fences. You must consider the speed you are to ride at, and gradually encourage the horse to jump certain fences at a faster pace as he gains confidence in what he is doing.

The Balanced Gallop
Your early training has taught the horse to relax when he gallops and to listen to your aids to shorten and lengthen the strides, and it has hopefully taught him to stay in a faster rhythm and speed without

Dance in the Dark sailing over a palisade

TAKE IT GENTLY

I believe very firmly that the horse must be quite confident, and must have learnt to jump the obstacles cleanly and in a relaxed manner, before a rider asks for much speed. Some people get away with riding their horses very fast over fences, but one day they will hit a fence hard or have a fall and the horse will lose all confidence. It is therefore well worth taking more time, as long as the rider tackles every fence positively; it is no good having a rider on a young horse who is not really convinced that he *does* want to get to the other side of each fence! Any young horse is bound to falter or be unsure on approaching a strange obstacle, and at this moment the rider's leg and seat aids must be quick, firm and positive, telling the horse that it is quite all right to negotiate it, in a quite definite, but unflustered manner.

taking too much out of himself by pulling and resisting the restraining aids. It is now time to put this into practice by taking the horse cross-country schooling, when you ride from fence to fence. He must listen to the restraining aids and learn to come back and be steady for such combinations as sunken roads, bank and rails, angled rails or bounces, but he must also be ready to move on when asked and to lengthen his stride in between the fences, and to jump the easier galloping fences on a longer stride. He has to learn to regulate his speed in between fences, too, and not to pull and fight when you ask him to shorten his stride before a particular fence or turn. If this happens, he must be taught that such behaviour is not what you want: canter at a reasonable speed and ask him to steady; if he fights he must be halted in a straight line and made to stand for a few moments, then let him go forwards to canter again quietly, lengthening the strides, then shortening them until he listens and respects the rider. Do not jump any fences until he is obedient, then

repeat the routine of jumping a few fences and making the horse steady and listen to your commands before jumping again.

It may take quite a while at home to teach your horse to stay in a balanced gallop, especially a thoroughbred which has perhaps come out of training and always expects to gallop for a long distance at considerable speed. However, this early training in faster work is very important, particularly for the cross-country, if you are going to have a fast and safe ride when jumping at speed. There are so many horses which get over-excited on the cross-country or in a jump-off, and they lose countless time faults and sacrifice accuracy because they take so long to listen to the rider who is having to fight for control before each fence, and much further out from the fence than if the horse was obedient and between hand and leg. It is a pleasure to watch the likes of Ginny Elliott (Leng) or Mark Todd whose horses are so beautifully balanced and obedient, qualities which really constitute the hallmark of their success.

To get a lazy horse to go forwards it is often a help to have a schoolmaster riding five strides ahead; this should help to get his blood up and encourage him to take up the rein contact through his own impulsion. The second time round let him go ahead over the same course at a rather faster pace so that he learns to enjoy it. After a few practice sessions like this the lazy horse should have bucked up his ideas, and you should expect him, after warming up, to move smartly from a standing start, to take up the contact and take on the course.

With the more excitable, forward-going type of horse you must be careful to keep him calmly and easily in balance, not to over-ride your fences, and to keep him relaxed, though without losing impulsion. There will be no need to practise standing starts with this type of horse; in fact it would be better to go gradually from halt, through walk, trot and then to canter and on to the first fence, without hurrying him unduly.

Jumping Over Water

Most people leave jumping over water until too late in the horse's training, probably because they don't have a suitable jump easily available. However, if you are seriously considering training horses for showjumping then a proper water jump is an investment you should consider; it will be invaluable for training your own horses, besides which you will be able to hire it out to others. A bit of spade-work and a polythene sheet will start you off and would be sufficient, before looking to a proper concrete construction with mats and so on. If jumping water is introduced at this stage in training, at a sensible width, then the horse has no problem in learning to cope with it easily, and to stretch and bascule over it; otherwise he will probably end up being rushed to the fence because he is spooking at it, with the result that he jumps flat and on the forehand.

A water jump is best introduced by building a triple bar over a small brush fence, with the water on the far side and under the triple bar. I don't usually show the horse the fence at all, but let him just take it in his stride; if he is really confident in his other jumping and doing related distances well, this should be no problem. Keep the water length about two metres (6½ft) to start with, increasing to three metres (10ft) when he is confident, and the highest rail over the water about a metre (3ft) high. If the horse jumps

WATER TRAYS

These are usually blue and made of rubber or painted plywood; they are approximately a metre (3ft 3in) wide and are generally positioned under a parallel or upright fence. A similar-looking obstacle can be made with fertiliser bags, for schooling purposes. If you can use proper trays, do not fill them with water until the horse is happily jumping over the fence with the tray underneath – be sure not to make the height of the fence too low or its width (with the tray beneath) will be out of proportion. Ride positively but not as forwards as when jumping open water. When the horse is happily jumping the trays dry, then put some water in them and continue as before; the water should have no effect on the horse provided you are positive about the way you ride the obstacle.

rather flat over the fence, then raise the poles until he jumps in a correct arc. When he is jumping this correctly, take away the middle rail, then the front rail, and later the farthest rail, until he is jumping just brush fence and water. If the horse loses his bascule over the water, then keep re-introducing your rail until he realises he must jump it in a correct shape. Also, ride the horse on in the last stride before a water jump very positively and forwards, so that he has a different feel from your legs than he would for a normal jump, to propel him forwards as well as upwards.

CROSS-COUNTRY FOR CATHERSTON HORSES

Catherston Humbug had his first cross-country schooling day with Catherston Dance in the Dark as schoolmaster; we first showed them some of the more spooky fences, and then jumped some small natural fences to start with. Lizzie was on Dance in the Dark giving Humbug a lead. Dance in the Dark took all

the island fences in his stride; being an older horse with more jumping experience he loved it all – until he came to the coloured barrels, which upset his easy rhythm the first time, although he jumped them much more fluently at the second attempt. Humbug followed over all the easy fences, and we then progressed to jumping down steps and over ditches. This went well, so we took each horse individually round a small course of jumps, some of which they had already seen and jumped, and some other new ones. They both learnt to settle into a steady gallop in between the fences, and appeared to enjoy themselves.

Humbug still has the occasional run-out, but with more practice I am sure this tendency will be resolved, when the horse has more confidence in what is being asked of him. He is only a four-year-old, and it will be at least another year before he is ready to start eventing; he will probably do some hunter trials later on in the year.

With another school or two, Dance in the Dark is really ready to start Pre-Novice events in the autumn. This horse is a real natural, and one which his rider will have to keep holding back on the cross-country as he is very bold and could easily over-jump; he won't need much fast-work training, either. He has a huge stride for a small horse and tremendous scope over a fence; we will have to take care at combination fences that he doesn't jump in too big and frighten himself by being too close to the next obstacle to jump out.

Dance in the Dark coming out of the wood jumping easily over a parallel, the first element of the combination (see overleaf)

The next stage: Dance in the Dark completes the combination by clearing a fence built of coloured barrels

RIDING CROSS-COUNTRY FENCES

Jumping into and out of Water

When the horse is confident about going into water at different places, and is happy to walk and trot into and through water – something we continue to practise throughout his education – you could build a small obstacle on the way out of the water so that he learns to enter it, trot through and then jump out. Then try it the other way, though first put the jump far enough away so that the horse can land on dry land before he enters the water. Build up his confidence gradually: thus when this is successfully negotiated, place the obstacle nearer to the edge of the water so that ultimately you have him jumping actually into and out of water. At a much later stage, and only when the horse is really confirmed in confidence about water, try jumping in down a bank, and eventually over a log on a bank into water; however, this is quite an advanced question to ask any young horse so early in his training. A log on the edge of a water is an ideal first jump into water, but it must have a simple approach.

Think of schooling into water as a totally normal exercise for your horse, so that when you get to your event there is nothing special about having to enter or jump into water, you will have done it so many times before. At a competition just ride into the water fence as you do in your training sessions, although you may need to use a little more leg as this is a different place and surrounding. *Do not* ride in the way you see so many riders carrying on – apparently consumed with worry,

This horse is jumping into the water boldly. He is a little tense and is therefore making rather too big a jump, but with more practice he will learn to relax and pop into water with less drive, making the whole jump and landing easier for both himself and his rider

This combination is jumping out of the water very cleanly and in good balance. Both are looking ahead for the next fence, and the whole attitude is forward thinking

they throw caution to the wind and get up speed, lose their rhythm and therefore unbalance their horse on the approach; this doesn't give the horse time to realise what is coming up next and he is thoroughly flustered by his rider's sudden total change in attitude and approach. He ends up going too fast into the fence, doesn't have time to appreciate what is in front of him, and arrives in the water with a huge splash, quite unbalanced and probably thoroughly alarmed as he makes his way out. This sort of riding will undermine any confidence the horse might have had in his rider, and at the next event when he suddenly goes into 'water attack' the horse is quite likely to stop – he will be confused and worried by his rider's attitude, and will remember from the last time that this approach upset him.

Always be aware that when you are jumping into water there will be a certain degree of drag, depending on its depth, with the effect that the front legs will slow down as the horse lands; you are therefore looking for the horse to jump neatly into the water at a controlled speed; you should keep your lower leg tight and close to the girth as for a drop fence, with your upper body in balance, and prepared for the horse possibly to slow down on entry to the water, and even to peck.

At one time I did quite a bit of eventing with Dutch Gold (Willow). On one occasion we were approaching a water complex, and as I had not done much schooling into water and knowing he was not very confident, I steadied up to trot; however, recollecting that I must ride positively, I clicked and closed my legs to encourage him forwards – and Willow changed gear so dramatically that we went from our nice working trot to a medium canter in two strides, followed by a big bold jump over the log and drop, and into the water with much more aplomb than I had intended! I am not sure that Willow realised it was water he was landing in, or maybe it was the speed with which we hit it, but we both went under! I came up gasping for air, to see Dutch Gold leaving the water! Oh no, loose stallion I thought, and called 'Willow, come here'. To my relief and amazement he turned round and trotted into the water, straight to me, and stopped. I remounted, and as I left the water to go to the next fence I heard the fence judge say, 'Now that's dressage for you!'. However, I am sure that Willow felt suddenly insecure on his own in a strange place and so was glad to come to a voice that he knew well, which was quite a relief to me as I was not looking forward to the long walk back to the lorry! Willow then had a few quiet training sessions to restore his confidence in water crossings and in me, and learnt to brace himself on entering the water, which he did at all the events that followed – and I learnt that his response to my aids could be similar to a Formula One car or a Lamborghini!

Ditches
Ditches in whatever shape or form always cause problems with horses, and you must be prepared to spend some considerable time teaching your horse to jump them. You may have already started this part of his education in the course of your hacking out, perhaps when you found a small natural ditch you wished to cross, probably with some mud or a little water in the bottom. This may have been only a foot wide, but it is the best way to start, and your horse should have learnt to walk and trot over ditches of this

type without fuss or panic.

The next step is to find a small, clearly defined ditch – or make one. A sleeper-faced (railroad tie) ditch is essential if you are making one up, especially on the take-off side. It is safer to leave it unfaced on the landing side in case the horse jumps awkwardly and fails to land clear when he could possibly slip and hurt himself on the sleeper. If possible I prefer a natural ditch anyway. Some bold horses will just follow an older experienced horse over a ditch, taking it in their stride: choose a ditch which is inviting, and follow at a balanced but positive canter, keep your leg on for the last few strides, but do not hurry the horse, and try to jump a ditch as if it were a fence – ditches should be jumped as if jumping an open water, except that rather than water there is a huge black-looking hole! Position yourself about three to four lengths behind your schoolmaster.

If your horse refuses at this big black hole then you must allow him time to have a good look, but insist that he doesn't turn away from it. Give him time to make his mind up that he *can* do it for himself; it does often help if your schoolmaster horse can come past you and pop over the ditch to keep reminding him that it is quite possible and a safe thing to do. When he does pluck up enough courage and jumps the ditch, be *extremely* careful not to catch him in the mouth by hanging on to the reins: let them slip through your fingers and gather them up again on landing, or hang on to the mane or a neck-strap. Then of course reward him, but go on and ask him to do it a few more times until he is quite relaxed and enjoying it all. Go to the same place a few days later and repeat the exercise until the horse is confident; then go to different places, by which time you should expect him to jump confidently.

Dance in the Dark jumping his first ditch

Dance in the Dark jumping his first coffin fence

Next you must introduce him to made-up ditches which are sleeper-faced and probably deeper. However, every stage must be worked through slowly and positively, and only you as his rider can assess when the horse is ready to go on and be faced with more demanding obstacles. It is always better to go more slowly than to push forwards too quickly and find he has lost his confidence in you.

The Coffin Combination

It was Dance in the Dark this time who was to do the learning: we wanted him to jump a combination fence of log, one stride to a ditch, one stride and another log. The ditch was no more than a metre (3ft) wide, but it was quite deep and dark, being sleeper-lined; so to start with we asked Dance in the Dark to

jump just the ditch alone. However, even this horse, who is very bold, found it rather uninviting and he jumped it awkwardly the first few times; but he was rewarded each time he jumped it, and soon gained confidence. When he was popping over the ditch easily, he was then ridden forwards, straight to the log, which he jumped well. We then turned him round and rode him positively over all three obstacles, and these he jumped very well once he understood what he was being asked to do.

Catherston Humbug, on the other hand, was convinced that there was a troll or an ogre in the bottom of this ditch that everybody was jumping! As I was on my feet, I led him up to the ditch which was so terrifying him, and stood over it. This gave the horse a lot of

confidence, and he sniffed at the edge for a while, and eventually became quite relaxed about this new, educational object. Lizzie then rode Humbug; after refusing a few times he jumped the ditch but then he went straight on and jumped the log out. We didn't ask him to jump the whole logs and ditch combination, as we felt that it was too early in his education.

The biggest cause of stops at this type of fence is the coffin built with post and rails, ditch and then another post and rail, as so often the horse can see the second post and rail as well as the ditch, and his concentration is therefore diverted from the first post and rail as he comes into it. As a rider you should make sure that the horse is listening to you, and that you really do have his attention: then ride the first element positively, and immediately ride forwards over the other two obstacles. At Novice level you will usually have one stride, perhaps even two, between the obstacles, but the nearer to Advanced you become, the more questions will be asked, such as a bounce which is quite difficult – there could also be a drop going in and a hill coming out! Most combination fences, from Novice through to Advanced level, will have an alternative route of some sort, so it is very important to walk your fence correctly, noting where all the flags are and where you can go if you have a stop somewhere within a combination fence.

Humbug jumping the coffin ditch, having first been given the chance to have a good look at it, which he did with a great deal of snorting. Because he was so inexperienced he was asked to jump only the ditch and log afterwards on that occasion, and was not expected to tackle the whole combination by jumping in over the log, too, as Dance in the Dark had done

Dance in the Dark jumping rails out of a wood, with a small drop landing: in this complex he had first jumped up a step, and then taken two strides to the rail – like a miniature Normandy bank

Drops and into Space

This type of fence is best introduced to the young horse's repertoire situated on just a slight slope, so he can see the landing as he is coming in to take off. I would start over a small, sloping triple-bar type fence which he could see through, so that he knew the ground was on the other side; once he understands this, the jump can be made into a solid fence, either a palisade or log so that when he comes into the fence he cannot see the other side. This particular type of fence is where the horse's trust in you is very important, as you are asking him to do something which is quite contrary to his instinct – a horse always likes to be able to see where he can land before he takes off. It is most important therefore that you have walked the fence well: don't ask too much of your horse by galloping into it, particularly as he might then jump too big and land too far down the slope, which could frighten him as well as jar his legs on landing. Rather, come into it on a bouncy stride, keeping the horse in front of you with your hands low and soft, and ready to slip the reins if necessary as he just pops down over the fence.

Banks and Steps

Steps and banks don't usually cause much trouble once the horse has learnt to jump down happily. To start with, find a steep gradient and make him descend it slowly, in good balance and in control of his own equilibrium; then turn round and trot up it, making sure that you are in the correct centre of gravity. When this is achieved easily, introduce an obstacle such as a log on a similar gradient, or small rails so that the horse has to jump and land on the gradient. The rider must stay in a balanced position and go

with the horse. Leaning back as you jump will give you an uncomfortable ride and is likely to unseat you; it is also uncomfortable for the horse and apt to make him hollow in the future. Maintain the normal jumping position, but with your lower leg firmly on the girth line or a little in front of it, to compensate for the drop landing.

Once the horse has learnt to jump sensibly over this obstacle, he is ready to start tackling bank-type fences. Steps up are easier to ride, as you approach them just like a fence, allowing the horse to jump on to the top of the bank and riding forwards on landing. At first he may find it strange to land on top of the bank, but he will soon adjust to the situation. Some horses find it harder to take the plunge downwards, so start with very little steps, not more than a sleeper high, so as to build up their confidence – it is easy at this height, but increase it gradually until you have a two- or three-sleeper drop. If the horse categorically refuses to take the plunge (which rarely happens if you start low enough) keep him facing in the required direction until he understands that nothing is going to harm him; eventually he will leap rather awkwardly forwards, and you must be prepared for this, staying in balance with him and not catching him in the mouth, and if necessary slipping the reins. It is a wise precaution when practising these fences for your horse to be wearing a neck-strap.

Catherston Humbug and Catherston Dance in the Dark's introduction to jumping steps went very successfully, and they both negotiated a small step confidently, having had a good look at it first. Humbug, being younger than Dance in the Dark, only did the one step down and up; Dance in the Dark is

a year older, so he went on a bit later to negotiate a series of three steps. They both looked rather circumspectly at the step down, so we asked them to drop down over it quietly a couple of times, which they did; then we asked them to jump up it, which they both did straightaway. We were also able to jump a small fence about six strides away through a wood, so could do the two in succession; it was quite helpful to be going on in canter towards the little step down, which they both popped down from canter. I called it a day with Humbug, who had been very good at this his first session of learning about steps; he had also learnt to jump a log with a drop landing, which he did easily, and altogether he appeared to have quite a lot of confidence for cross-country fences which was encouraging for the future.

Dance in the Dark jumping sensibly up a small bank

Left:
Humbug inspecting his first small drop; he then pops down very calmly

Dance in the Dark jumping a sequence of three steps down for the first time – quite a test for a young horse. However, he was quick to work out what he had to do, and coped very neatly down these big steps

Lizzie continued with Dance in the Dark to some of the more advanced fences, which included the three bigger steps down. He popped down the first one very neatly, but was taken rather by surprise at the second, launching himself off and veering rather to the left before

taking on the third step; this was one stride away, so he had a bit of room to organise himself and popped down neatly. On the next attempt he was much tidier, and being a horse that loves a challenge, gave a little buck afterwards as if to say 'What a clever boy I am!'.

BEHAVIOUR IN THE START BOX
We have had several horses who were difficult to start in the box with previous riders. We found that with a calm, quiet rider who didn't get het up, any of these horses would walk into the start box and start quite easily, provided they were kept steadily between leg and rein and went quietly into canter when asked to start.

Bank and Rails
Ride these as you would a step up, or a series of steps up. Approach in a bouncy canter with lots of impulsion for the effort of the step up, and depending whether there is a stride or a bounce on the top, ride firmly forwards for the required effort. If there is a drop on the landing side of the rails you should be prepared for this by keeping your lower leg firm on the girth and being ready to slip your reins. Some horses, when they realise there is a drop, may try to fiddle an extra stride on the top; this will put them under the fence, however, and will make the landing after the drop slower but steeper. A horse which does this regularly may well have some kind of underlying front leg problem or soreness, or it may have been frightened in the past; whatever the reason, it should be ridden more strongly for the correct stride so it doesn't land too steeply the other side of the fence. Sometimes there is a large ditch at the bottom, and a horse that doesn't jump this type of fence properly may end up in it.

Sunken Road
This combination involves steps down and up, with one or two strides across the road in the bottom, and there may be a fence before the step down and another after the step up. Your horse must therefore be well balanced and full

of impulsion on the approach, but don't rush him because he must be allowed to jump cleanly and softly over all the elements; your riding must be positive, especially on landing in the road, as the horse must realise he has to respond to the jump up the step as well as taking on the fence following it. Make sure that he is concentrating on the step up, too, and not just looking to the fence further on.

Angled Rails, Bounces and Corners
These are often built as one fence at a Novice event, and the rider has to make the decision as to which part of it to jump. This will depend on your horse, his way of going, and how successfully you can ride him straight between your leg and rein. If this sort of complex occurs early in the course the horse may not be going forwards well enough to cope with the bounce or the corner; and if it comes in the middle or towards the end of the course you may be galloping on and prefer to do the corner rather than collecting for the bounce or having to steer for the angled rails, generally a longer approach which wastes time. This type of fence can be constructed at home using blocks and rails, and if you have enough material you can make a corner and a bounce and even the angled rails on the end.

When jumping angled rails, aim to take the straightest route across the widest part of each fence, therefore taking each one at a slight angle. Ideally you want to make the angles as slight as possible but also the route as direct as possible so that you are not pulling your horse around and unbalancing him.

To ride a bounce, collect your horse into a short, athletic canter. This does not want to be done miles away from the fence as this will waste time and energy, and your horse will probably have lost his momentum by the time he gets to it. Nor should you allow the horse to gallop into the fence and then suddenly ask him to collect, which he may not be willing to do if he has seen the fence in front of him. On your approach to a bounce fence you should ask the horse for a few half-halts in the gallop to make him pay attention to you, and then about eight strides away from the fence collect him into your short, bouncy canter. From here, keep your leg on and ride the horse into the fence, staying in balance and following his movement. As this is not a bounce fence that he knows, you may have to ride slightly more forwards in the middle of the fence than you would when practising at home.

The corner element of this fence should only be jumped if your horse is going correctly forwards between hand and leg and is good and obedient to steer. As regards impulsion it should be jumped like any normal parallel. To jump a corner with an accurate and safe line you should think of it as a V and then draw a straight line from the point of the V to another point equidistant between the two ends; aim to ride straight at this line so as to cross it at right-angles and as close to the point of the corner as is safe. When you walk the course, work out where your line should start from and where you are aiming; if you are walking the course with a friend, get him or her to stay out in the open on your route from the last fence while you walk up to the corner, looking all the time for your line over the fence, and for a landmark to aim at on the far side of the fence, such as a tree or telegraph pole. Make sure that your friend stays in the same place until you have worked out exactly where you are going to jump and are happy with your line of approach!

TOWARDS COMPETITION

Our event horse is now ready to start his final fittening programme before his first proper event, and our showjumping horse is also ready, having accomplished most of the above training exercises: the event horse had obviously been gaining useful experience for his eventing career; the showjumper will have acquired a wealth of knowledge and a certain capability for self-preservation which will stand him in good stead for his showjumping career. More and more showgrounds nowadays have certain natural hazards incorporated into the course, such as the 'Devil's Dyke' at Hickstead, and enclosed table fences when you jump up on to a platform bank, and after a stride or two, jump off down a drop; sometimes a hedge may be incorporated into a jump. The dressage horse will have learnt not to be neurotic!

It is entirely up to you as to how much cross-country schooling you wish your dressage horse to do; if he shows a lot of talent over fences, I consider it is good for his education and teaches him to cope with different going and to balance himself in different situations. After a time, however, the dressage horse becomes so valuable that you may not wish to risk him jumping very much, as his fitness requirement for dressage does involve using different muscles as he becomes more advanced. His temperament and type will dictate how much fast work you need to do to keep him suitably fit in his heart, lungs and wind for the standard of dressage test he is performing.

Chapter 8

Preparing for Competition

Whether you plan a schooling session or to go to a small competition, you will almost certainly have to get there by lorry or trailer, so the young horse must learn all about motor transport!

TRAVELLING

For a few days before you actually go anywhere, you should practise dressing him up as if you were going to load him, with travelling boots or bandages, knee caps, and possibly hock boots, too, so that he can get used to the feel of them. He may kick out because they feel strange so he should be walked about in them until he gets used to them. If he continues to fuss, make sure that the straps are correctly adjusted but then he should be verbally reprimanded. Only when the horse is quite accustomed to all this clothing should you attempt to load him into the lorry.

Loading and Unloading

Place the vehicle close to a fence or building on the right-hand side (this leaves a side ramp, usually on the left-hand side of a lorry or trailer, unobstructed should you want to open it) and make the ramp as shallow as possible; it must be firm and should not move about when you tread on it. A loading ramp, if

available, is usually a great asset and often minimises the chances of frightening the horse which may cause problems in the future. Ultimately, of course, the horse has got to learn to walk up a proper lorry ramp, but this is a good way to start, and he can learn to walk up and down the loading ramp nearly on the flat before he tackles the added problem of a slope. If the lorry or trailer has a side or front ramp it is a help if this can be opened to give more light in the vehicle.

Don't give the horse any feed for a few hours so that he really appreciates his reward when he gets into the vehicle. Put a little straw on the ramp to make it look more inviting. If it is a big lorry, it is often a help to let the young horse see another horse load up and stand in it; this is not advisable in a trailer, however, as you will probably want to move the partition to make the entrance as large as possible. Have a bucket of feed ready in the vehicle, so the horse can see it, to reward him once he has gone in.

Always put a bridle on the horse over his headcollar and have a long rope or lunge rein attached either to a coupling or through the near-side bit-ring and attached to the off-side ring. Take the horse to the ramp and let him have a look at what you are going to ask him to do. When he has had a good sniff at the ramp, turn him round and ask him to walk forwards and into the vehicle. If he is nervous, don't hurry, but walk up the ramp a fair way yourself so that he can see it is safe. Give him time to investigate the ramp, then ask him in a firm, positive way to walk up it. He may falter at the edge of the ramp, so pick up a front foot and place it on the ramp and ask him to walk forwards again. If he is still reluctant, an assistant could come alongside and encourage him forwards quietly with a schooling whip, but *without* hitting him. If you are making no progress, stand and wait for a time, then turn the horse round and walk forwards again. If he persists in stopping at the bottom, now is the time to use a lunge rein to assist you.

The method I prefer is to make a loop with the buckle end of the lunge rein which slips over the quarters of the horse with the buckle on top of the loins; the remaining end of the lunge rein runs down his back on the near side of his withers and neck and threads through the throatlash and noseband of the headcollar to your hand. Use this rein with short pulls, and the horse always seems to come to you. If he starts to run backwards give him a few tweaks of the rein, and as soon as he comes forwards lighten your feel. A few minutes with this method – provided you haven't got the horse already into a stew by chasing it with whips – and he will walk up to you in a confident and happy manner. Eventually he will walk into the vehicle, though be prepared to spend some time trying!

Once he is in, reward him with some feed and let him stay there for a time, or even take him for a short drive. Take care when shutting the partitions that you don't frighten him, and be sure to close the ramp slowly.

When a horse comes out of the lorry for the first time it is often advisable to have two people to keep him straight and to make him walk down the ramp slowly. In a trailer, great care must be taken to prevent the horse hitting his head on the roof as you load and unload, as any such trauma will make things very difficult for the future. *Never* pull on a horse's head, either when you are trying to make him go into a trailer, or when he is coming out backwards from one; and be careful not to let him slip off the edge of the ramp when he is backing out as this will make him nervous.

Loading Problems

I have experienced a number of difficulties with regard to loading, although most of our young horses learn to load and unload when foals and yearlings and usually we don't have any problems after that. However, there is many a horse that comes here for a lesson or to stud and then doesn't appear to want to go home! I did once have a foal (eight months old and therefore fairly big!) who defeated three of us by just lying down on the ramp of the trailer and refusing to move. One of us was holding the mare in the trailer, but in fact that made no difference at all as the foal was ready to be weaned and quite independent, and therefore not too concerned if he did his own thing and mum went somewhere else; so we weaned him there and then, rolling him off the ramp and leaving him in the field while we took mum away! The next day we went back with reinforcements so we were five people to the one foal, and in fact it was so delighted to see us that it walked straight into the trailer with hardly a second thought!

I try not to get involved with other people's horses and ponies that

Equiment: Travelling

Headcollar
Ropes (2)
Travel boots, or bandages with gamgee of Fibergee under them
Knee caps
Hock boots
Cooler rug
Day rug
Tail bandage
Tail guard
Overreach boots (4)
(if a poor traveller)
Haynet (1 full)
Water bucket
Water container
Hard feed

*Loading and unloading
the young horse*

*Stand by the lorry and
reassure the horse by
moving on and off the
ramp while getting him
ready. Always have a
bridle and headcollar on
the horse for extra control.
The horse must realise that
he must only do what he
is told, and that he will
get a reward when he is in
the lorry*

*Most horses do not walk
readily into a lorry on the
first try, and I use a
method given to me by a
cowboy which is easy to
handle single-handed, and
which is usually successful.
This three-year-old filly is
just backed, and is rather
reluctant to enter the lorry.
Make a loop with the
lunge rein, and drop the
loop over the quarters.
Thread the rest of the rein
through the throat-latch
and noseband of the
headcollar. This is
sufficient for most horses,
but if one is headstrong or
particularly nervous, also
run a lunge rein through
the near-side bit-ring*

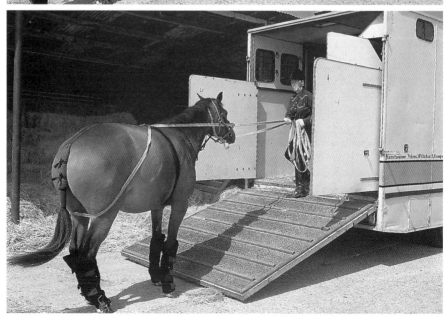

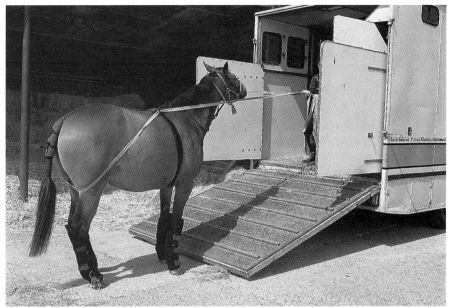

Lead the horse to the edge of the ramp, with a normal long lead-rein. Allow the horse to examine and sniff the ramp; if it wants to back away give it a little tweak forwards with the lunge rein, and each time it moves a little forwards release the rein behind its quarters and reward it with your voice. Continue the little sharp jerks until the horse walks up the ramp, and then position it in the lorry and reward it with some food. Take your time, and never rush the horse

When unloading, it is useful to have an assistant to help keep the horse straight and make it walk slowly down the ramp, as shown here. Practise loading and unloading at home until the horse is confident and you should have no trouble at a show or event. Remember to avoid accidents; put leg protectors on the horse so that it does not hurt itself on the edge of the ramp, and make sure it does not hit its head on the roof of the lorry or trailer. The method of loading described here does help to keep the horse's head down

will not load, but if they are here at stud or schooling, you are really obliged to help! The method described on p147 with the looped lunge line has nearly always worked, and furthermore does not put you too much at risk as you are in front of the horse and well away from his body and hind legs; all you need is a clear route backwards into the lorry or trailer. In really bad cases I have made a small enclosure round the back of the ramp using jump poles and blocks, then if the horse does go backwards he will hit himself on the poles; this makes him cautious so he does everything much more slowly.

There are many other methods that can be used: some people use lunge lines, others whips or brooms; some join hands behind a horse's backside and push like the racehorse-stall loaders do; some blindfold him with coats or stable rubbers, and others try to back horses in. Whichever method you use, you must always keep calm and not lose your temper – we all know there is nothing more frustrating than having had a bad day and then the horse will not load. Dare I say it, but patience and boredom may well win the day, and if you all sit down on the ramp and have a relax and a rest and keep the horse waiting at the bottom of the ramp, then inquisitiveness and boredom may well help get him in! I, however, will always stand by my time-honoured lunge-rein method, taught to me by a cowboy many years ago.

Gaining Experience
Leave the horse in the lorry for half an hour or so, remaining nearby so as to talk to him should he become nervous, giving him a reassuring pat or a little bit of food. When he has settled and is evidently not going to fuss and get worried you can tie up

a haynet. You can also give him a drink from a bucket, especially if your stables have automatic water bowls, as a bucket will seem new and different in these circumstances and you do not want him to go thirsty at his first show. A little cut grass will always help the horse enjoy being in the lorry and make him look forward to his time there.

Once the horse has learnt how to load and unload it is always a good idea to take him on a little outing, say to a friend where you can ride him in different surroundings. It would be helpful to hack him out, perhaps with your friend's horse so that he has company. Take him to work in a strange arena, indoors or outdoors; use the showjumps which will obviously be different from the ones you have been using, also any cross-country fences if available, logs or any other different terrain which you may be able to train him over. You would be wise to take your horse out on several trips like this before you can consider him travelled enough to go for any serious outing, such as a proper training session for example, or a clear round jumping, an unaffiliated dressage competition or a cross-country school.

FITNESS WORK

The dressage horse will be basically quite fit from the general training he has been having since he was broken in, that is of hill work, hacking out, an occasional canter and general schooling and education. This level of fitness will be quite sufficient for competition.

The young showjumper is also probably quite fit in general, although he should be training in particular for jumping twice a week. He should have hill work or cantering once a week when out hacking to keep his wind clear, and general flatwork schooling for the remaining three days. Having progressed through early training over single fences, doubles and grids his muscles and frame will be quite jumping fit, but during these further jumping sessions not only will he need to continue this gymnastic work, he should also jump full courses, and start working towards jump-off techniques. This should *not* involve pulling him sharply round the corners into his fences as the top international horses are able to do, because he is not sufficiently advanced in his training; it is more a question of keeping him balanced in a good working to medium canter, and training him to jump at a slightly faster speed than he would normally so that he is not fazed by this when you go to your first show and hopefully qualify for the jump-off! Read your schedule carefully, as some classes now have the jump-off course immediately following the first round (A5); if this is the case, your horse should be prepared and fit enough for this, as it could mean jumping about seventeen fences, one after the other!

Training Programme for a Jumper

Event horses do need a higher level of fitness than showjumpers, and although the young horse will be reasonably fit, six weeks before your first 'proper' event you should begin a proper fittening programme. It is advisable to find out which event would be most suitable as a start for your young horse, as some courses are easier and better suited to a first-timer than others; also find out if the course is very hilly or reasonably flat, as your horse will need to be really much fitter for a hilly course – you don't want him to

tire and risk him making a silly mistake because of this. Therefore in your programme you are having to incorporate your flatwork, athletic jumping, hacking and hill work, and your fast canter work, including a cross-country schooling session.

Interval Training

I have always used the traditional way of getting a horse fit for an event, that is of gradually building up the work, the distance and the speed as you get nearer to the event. Nowadays there are many new methods and techniques and programmes, such as interval training for fittening horses which is being used by many successful

---

A POSSIBLE WEEKLY ROUTINE FOR A SHOWJUMPER

A four-week programme before your first 'proper' jumping show might be as follows:

Monday: 45-min hack, walking and trotting, followed by 30-min flatwork schooling, working particularly on transitions from one pace to another and transitions within the paces, lengthening and collecting the strides, decreasing and increasing the size of circles.

Tuesday: 30-min hack, followed by jumping training, including trotting poles, gridwork and individual fences.

Wednesday: 60-min hack including hill work incorporating some schooling exercises of obedience such as shoulder-in, leg-yielding, lengthening and shortening the strides, walk-to-canter and canter-to-walk transitions.

Thursday: 30-min hack and a half mile at half-speed canter, working to a mile by week 4. Walk for 20 min on the way home.

Friday: As Monday.

Saturday: Similar to Tuesday, but jumping should be of individual fences and a course, possibly with a jump-off session.

Sunday: Day off, turn out, graze in hand or hack out quietly at walk for 30 to 40 min.

The above routine can be followed for the four weeks leading up to the show, gradually increasing the intensity of the work by week 4.

Fast work! Dance in the Dark following Humbug at a good half-speed gallop

competitors. Personally, I hate to see a horse finish an event with trembling legs, as when he is in this sort of state his muscles are very stressed and there is a high risk of breaking him down, as well as causing muscle damage. Interval training works on the principle of a short sharp work session of a few minutes, followed by a rest session of a couple of minutes until the horse's breathing and heart rate are nearly back to normal, followed by another short sharp work session and so on, building up the times of each session. However, beware: it is quite easy to overdo these sessions, and this could cause slight muscle

damage which may well go unnoticed.

My other concern with this form of fast-work fittening is that the horse is working hard for only short lengths of time – when later on you have a longer course or different terrain to cope with such as hills or bad going, it may easily cause him undue strain because he is only used to doing his set 'time' session before he has a rest. The principles of interval training lend themselves ideally to the fitness programme of a showjumper, which jumps a round and usually has a chance to rest before jumping another round for the jump-off; as the horse becomes

more experienced he will have to jump longer courses and exert himself more, but the period of exertion will still not be as long or strenuous as a cross-country course for the event horse.

Swimming

For horses which have a slight leg problem, or if the going is very hard and you do not wish to give your horse fast ridden work until it eases, then you could book a session at an equine swimming pool. Swimming works a horse's heart, lungs, muscles and legs without concussion of any kind and can be a useful form of training – but be careful, as the horse can become very fit, very quickly. A horse will not swim for long, but even a short spell of swimming works *all* a horse's muscles and is similar to a 40-min school or a good gallop. After a swimming session it is important that an event horse has a cross-country school into water to make sure that he will still brace himself for landing – otherwise he may associate all water with going for a swim! I am sure we made this mistake with Wellingtonia; she crumpled on landing in water after she had been swimming, so we are now always careful to do some water obstacles before the next event.

The lists below will probably terrify you, but it is better to be safe and prepared than sorry!

Equipment: Dressage

Horse
Saddle, girth, stirrups and 3 numnahs (saddle pads)
Bridle
Lunge rein
Cavesson
Lunge whip
Side-reins
Exercise boots
Schooling whip
Grooming kit
Water buckets (2), sponges and scraper
Water container (full)
Haynet (2 full)
Hard feed (as required, and take manger)
Studs and stud kit
Bridle number
Vaccination certificate which undeniably relates to the horse
First-aid kit for horse and rider
Sweat rug/cooler and waterproof sheet
Spare dry day rugs
Spare headcollar and ropes
Spare bridle

Rider
Hat (BSI or ASTM standard)

Training Programme for an Event Horse

A six-week preparation for a one-day event could be based on the following fortnightly programme:

Monday: 45-min hack, walking and trotting, followed by 30-min flatwork schooling, working particularly on transitions from one pace to another and transitions within the paces, lengthening and collecting the strides, circles, turns, trot-to-halt and halt-to-trot transitions and easy lateral work.

Tuesday: 30-min hack, followed by warm-up on the flat, then jumping training, including trotting poles on a circle, and gridwork incorporating bounces to one- and two-stride combinations.

Wednesday: 60-min hack including hill work incorporating some schooling exercises of obedience such as shoulder-in, leg-yielding, lengthening and shortening the strides, walk-to-canter and canter-to-walk transitions.

Thursday: 30-min hack and a half mile at half-speed canter, working to a mile by week 3, and one and a half miles by week 5, increasing the speed for the last quarter mile to three-quarter speed. Walk for 20 min on the way home.

Friday: As Monday.

Saturday: 20-min warm-up, followed by a cross-country schooling session in which a course of six to seven fences should be ridden at cross-country speed. Rest in walk for 10 min and then ride another short course.

Sunday: Day off, turn out, graze in hand or hack out quietly at walk for 30 to 40 min.

Monday: As the previous Monday, but work for a longer time in trot and canter in your schooling session, sometimes asking for smaller circles to balance the horse, serpentines, loops and some counter-canter.

Tuesday: 60-min hack including hill work in both trot and canter. Lengthening the strides, also staying in canter for a 5-min stint, building up to 10 min by week 6.

Wednesday: 30-min hack on roads and tracks, followed by flatwork schooling session in an arena with markers, running through different individual movements in the dressage test and practising the halts and other test transitions at the markers.

Thursday: 15-min hack, 15-min schooling session working on shortening and lengthening the canter, followed by a showjumping session with a course of fences.

Friday: 30-min hack, followed by a flatwork schooling session of 30 min in weeks 2 and 4, and 20 min in week 6, and then a sharp canter – in week 6 this should be only of a half mile at three-quarter speed (this would be just a 'pipe-opener' in preparation for the competition the following day).

Saturday: Travel to lesson with your trainer on the flat or for showjumping; in weeks 2 and 4 take horse to a clear round showjumping session. In week 6 this will be your 'proper' event.

Sunday: Trot up in hand to check for soundness, and perhaps walk to river and stand in water for 20 mins; then allow to graze, or turn out so can relax.

PREPARATIONS FOR THE FIRST COMPETITION

Before you can enter any affiliated competition both the rider and the owner of the horse must be paid-up members of the British Horse Society, or the American Horse Shows Association (AHSA) in the United States, and the horse must be registered with the relevant association or group. On joining you will receive the relevant rule book which you should read from cover to cover as there is a lot of information that you will need to know.

Dealing with an Over-excited Horse

Some horses are highly strung and always get very excited when they go to a new place and it may be advisable to lunge this sort when you arrive and before you ride him, especially if you are not feeling very brave! I would also tack him up completely in the lorry: saddle, bridle, side-reins (looped back to the D on the saddle and at the correct length) and exercise boots all round, lunge whip and a lunge line put through the near-side bit-ring and over the horse's head to the off-side bit-ring.

You should already have earmarked a quiet corner in which you can lunge him, so take him firmly and quietly to this area and put the side-reins on straightaway as he will only get wild and silly if he is not controlled right from the beginning. If he wants to canter or trot to start with, let him do so, though sensibly; then when he is tired and a bit quieter, ask him for transitions and so on. Don't even try to start in walk as this is bound to end in argument which will only make matters worse, and what is more will be remembered for the future; work in trot, and even canter. The horse must, of course, be used to wearing side-reins when he is lunged – if he is not, and has never worn them when schooling at home, do not put them on now! If he continues to be disobedient and excitable then continue lungeing him for at least half an hour.

Once he has calmed down and is listening to your commands it may be helpful to have an assistant to hold him while you mount, and also to lead you forwards on to the circle on which you have been lungeing him. When you feel that he is reasonably relaxed, then go forwards into trot on the lunge until you feel confident that he will be sensible when let off the lunge; hopefully this will be after only a few circuits. In fact all this is usually unnecessary, and anyway it is preferable not to have to lunge a young horse too much – the sooner you can mount up and ride him, the better.

When you start to ride a young horse in company introduce him to the other horses gradually, getting nearer just little by little; keep his concentration and make him listen to you by riding in trot in circles, through turns and on to straight lines, so he has no option but to listen to your commands. It is much safer to ride a horse forwards into trot than to keep him at walk, because if he does play up in walk he is more likely to rear, whereas in trot at least you can ride him forwards, and the more forwards he is ridden the less he can buck.

Having introduced the horse to this new environment then work him as you would expect to ride him in, up to a contact and working well from behind and through his back. When he is attentive and obedient take him to other parts of the field and get him nearer to where he is to perform, whether it is to have his lesson or to compete.

Perhaps you plan to do some clear-round jumping, in which case make sure that he is sensible before you attempt to jump the practice fence, because if he is still feeling fresh you may well be jumped off! Always start in trot, and use a placing pole as this will make him concentrate on the fence and help him to make a better approach.

Dressage continued

Jacket
Shirt
Tie or stock with pin
Breeches
Boots
Spurs
Gloves
Hairnet
Change of clothes/overalls
Waterproofs
Registration cards: rider, owner and horse

Equipment: Showjumping

As above, plus:
Jumping whip
Breastplate or breastgirth
Surcingle
Over-reach boots
Tendon boots
Running martingale (optional)

Equipment: Horse Trials

As above, plus:
Medical card and holder and number bib
Bandages or boots for cross-country
Cross-country bit or bridle, if necessary
Cross-country colours
Crash hat
Back protector
String gloves
Stopwatch

ON ARRIVAL AT THE COMPETITION

There are a number of things to do before you start with your horse:

For a dressage competition you should go to the secretary and declare that you are there, and check your times. Some competitions require to see your horse's vaccination certificate and registration card, especially if you have booked overnight stabling.

For showjumping competitions you should report to the secretary to collect your number; check which class is in progress, and work out when you will be able to walk the course for your class.

For horse trials you will need your horse's vaccination certificate because it must be checked before you are allowed to collect your number; you must also show your medical card in case you have had a fall recently.

After jumping, ride positively forwards and away from the fence, and steady him gradually, back to trot. If the horse is fresh it is better not to jump too much in the practice ring; he will concentrate better in the clear-round jumping ring, where he will not be distracted by other horses.

Some horses become really highly excited and never settle at all. I have found it best to work this sort for a good hour to an hour and a half, after which I dismount, wash him down and make him comfortable with a rug on; I then take him near to the other horses but at a safe distance, and allow him to graze for an hour, in the hope that he found pleasure from relaxing. I would then tack him up and ride him again, in walk and trot, trying to get him to settle down. If this still does not work after persevering for a few hours, I would take him home and let him unwind overnight in a small paddock, with a New Zealand rug on if it is wet.

I would then take him out again the next day, hopefully to the same place, and I am quite sure that he

would be feeling slightly subdued and would behave himself. If he does behave, then I would ride him for a short time, let him graze and make much of him. He can then go home to bed – but you will have to remember that this sort of horse needs to be taken to many different venues to get him used to going out. He may need to have the protein cut down in his feed, too, and he will probably be better if he is 'let down' a bit before you go to your first competition. Sometimes this sort is better turned out the night before a show, until he has learnt to grow up and accept the routines and situations asked of him. Dutch Gold used to get over-excited early in his career, and only by letting him down whilst still taking him to shows did he settle to his work. After a week or so of taking him to every local outing he settled down, and realised it was not so exciting after all.

Dealing with a Lazy Horse

Other horses are very lazy and laid back about going away from home, and never show any enthusiasm. They need a diet which is high in protein and low in carbohydrates, therefore only a little hay but lots of oats may help to perk them up. At a competition it is vital to keep their interest, with lots of upward and downward transitions; work them in short bursts and not for too long overall, and give plenty of rest periods in walk. Before actually competing, sharpen them up by extending and collecting the steps in trot and canter before going into the arena. You will have to ride this type of horse positively forwards in the arena, and give him plenty of reward when he goes well. If you are keeping him for dressage, a cross-country school or a small jump may brighten up his day and give him more 'oomph' for the future.

The Young Horse in Competition

You will have some idea of how your horse is going to behave when on an outing, having taken him cross-country schooling and to winter indoor competitions or lessons, though you must be aware that the horse is considerably fitter now and will therefore take a longer time to settle in most cases. If he is a very hot and excitable type then a few days before you go to your first competition I would turn him out as much as possible; I find a night in the field makes a tremendous difference to an excitable sort, even if you do have to get him in early, plait him up and get him ready just before loading up for the competition. It is better to have the horse less corned up and fit but thoroughly relaxed at this first show than having him feeling pent up and therefore a more tense ride to deal with, which will not leave him a good memory of competitions.

THE FIRST COMPETITIVE EVENT

When you arrive, find out where the correct ring is for your class, then unload your horse. It may be a good idea to tack him up in the lorry; it is certainly important to have put the bridle on, as he will probably be rather excitable in a strange place and may be more difficult to bridle outside, and you don't want to lose control and let go of him

With a lazy type, treat him as if this were a normal day; the only difference that he will experience is that on the actual day of the competition his routine will be upset by starting earlier – he will be fed earlier, and be plaited up and groomed before being prepared for travelling. It is important that you arrive in plenty of time before you are due to ride, ideally three hours before your first class or test; the horse can then get used to all the noises of the show, the loudspeakers, hustle and bustle and so on, whilst he is still in the lorry or trailer, and you will still have plenty of time to work him in and find out how he is going to react among so many other horses. You may find your quiet and sometimes lazy horse suddenly has a changed character and is now spooky, alert and showing off to all his new friends, pulling your arms out and making you feel as if you are sitting on a plank or on an unexploded bomb! In this case I would take him as far away as possible from the other horses and work him in trot and canter for at least half an hour non-stop until he is more subdued and is pleased to come back to walk.

When he has had time to relax and take stock of the situation then ride him up to the bridle, and when he is more sensible in trot, gradually introduce him to the other horses;

LUNGEING AT A SHOW

If the facilities allow at the show you are attending, you may like to lunge your horse before you get on him; with some young entires it is often preferable to do this as they are inclined to be fairly insufferable for the first five minutes anyway. I would always lunge with side-reins in this case, too, so that you have more control over him when he is at his most excitable. It is best to lunge well away from other horses, and only you can tell how long you need to lunge him – it will depend on the way he is behaving on the day.

work him as you would normally, though try not to get too close to any other horse so that you avoid upsetting either yours or another rider's. One excitable horse will very readily upset others, and it is fairly anti-social of you if you don't try to take control of yours and move away from the others if you are still having trouble.

Riding In

You will, if you have followed the above, have a quiet horse to ride now, but you may need to make him obedient and to keep him concentrating so you must think of your basic work. Start by riding him through transitions from trot to walk, walk to trot and trot to halt, and perform these intensively on a circle, for example. If he is still not really listening to you properly, then intersperse these transitions with some shoulder-in, and even travers on a circle so that he learns to listen to your leg aids. If you have a very excitable horse it is unwise to ask him to stand still for any length of time as this will make him feel even more explosive; it is better to keep him moving and his mind occupied, though with simple things that he knows how to do easily, and when he is a little more relaxed give him a longer rein and let him stretch within the pace he is in during his work. If he will walk on a long rein, then this is also relaxing. With a lazier type of horse you need to be rather sharper, and to encourage him forwards by asking for some extended paces and then some collected ones so that he is never sure what you are going to ask him to do and remains attentive and alert.

For dressage, work in as near to

the dressage arenas as possible, because this will accustom your horse to the differing types of arena boards and markers and will help him to settle in this area. When he has worked well and settled down it is also helpful to allow him to walk on a long rein and relax in this area. Make sure that you are correctly dressed at least five minutes before you are to enter the arena, and remove your horse's boots. Most

horses are better for doing a little trot and canter work just prior to going in, and it is always helpful to trot around the outside of the arena whilst waiting for the judge's bell.

For a showjumping competition it will probably not be possible to ride around the outside of the arena, and there will probably only be a collecting ring with practice fences in it for you to warm up over. The practice fences must only be jumped

Catherston Jetstream on her first round at Langford Horse Show. Here she is jumping very big and looks a bit anxious as it is her first show. She is almost jumping too quickly

in the direction indicated, that is with the red flag on your right and the white flag on your left. It is not permitted to raise these fences higher than the fences for the class in the ring at the time.

For horse trials, follow the above procedure for those two phases; then in addition you will have to warm up over the practice cross-country fence, which should be provided near the start of the cross-country course. A faster canter will focus the horse's mind on to the job in hand, and will work up both his and your adrenalin. Take care not to let him get cold immediately before you start the cross-country; sometimes you can be waiting for quite a long time if there has been a hold-up on the course, so have a rug available should you need it, and keep him walking.

The Dressage Test

Check with the steward how many horses there are to go before you, and if the class is running on time. Also check if a horn or bell is being used, and if there are several rings try to work out which horn is the sound for your ring. Take off your horse's boots now, too, as these are easily forgotten and to leave them on would mean elimination. Before you start, listen for the judge's horn or bell and on no account enter any part of the arena from any angle other than when you start your test by entering at A. If you are competing indoors, then check with the steward how you are to ride into the arena, whether you are allowed to enter the test area, or if you have to remain outside the test area if there is room.

You will have warmed up your

Catherston Dance in the Dark warming up for his first dressage competition, showing good balance

horse, and then will probably have time for a few minutes' quiet – having allowed for him to be slightly fresh at a new place – although you mustn't now let him go to sleep! You must have him going well forwards before you enter the arena. Many a time we have all heard the tale that the horse was going beautifully outside when warming up, and then 'died' when he entered the arena. Was this because when you stopped for the few minutes' break the horse thought he had stopped for the day? When this happens the rider must find extra reserves of energy to create the impulsion required from the horse in just the few moments it takes to get to the test arena. Again, you must create this impulsion after you have entered at A and as you trot down the centre line towards the judge. Energy and resolve: this is the way you create the best from your horse to make a test.

You will have memorised the correct test well before the competition, so you will know what is coming next and where you are going, and this means you can prepare your horse for the movements well in advance of them happening. It is no use thinking that you have a 20m circle at C when you arrive there, or that there is an upward or downward transition as you are on the marker. Preparation is required at least twenty metres before each movement, even if it is just getting your brain in order before you actually apply the aids. A 20 x 40m arena is small enough as it is, so use the whole arena and make sure you go into the corners correctly. The only exception to this rule might be if the weather conditions have been terrible and the track is like a quagmire, when you might try and pick a route either outside or inside the track.

TAKE CARE
Always remember to keep calm; think ahead for where your next movement is going to start. Keep the horse balanced and moving forwards. Remember to make a proper corner with the correct bend, and also to make your circle round, the right size and with the correct bend.

Remember that every movement starts when your body passes the marker, therefore make your circles round, and start and end at the marker required. Make turns and corners with the correct bend, and ride away in a straight line whilst still maintaining the horse's balance with the inside leg and outside rein. Serpentines should have even loops and should be accurately ridden; diagonals and straight lines should be ridden positively forwards and straight to the opposite marker.

If all should not go according to plan and you forget the test or your horse sees gremlins on the floor, do not panic but quietly keep your cool. If you have gone wrong, the judge will toot the horn or ring the bell. If you are totally confused as to what you have done, go to the judge and ask what you should be doing, and hopefully the rest of the test will come back to you. If the gremlins are alive and your horse is spooking at every marker, blade of grass or glint of sunlight, you must try and keep his attention by riding him nearly in shoulder-in past each respective gremlin, then allow him to go straight again. Don't forget the importance of using your leg before your hand to keep him straight between the reins, and as soon as he responds to your correcting aids then lighten the feel on the rein as soon as you can, to help make him relax. Always remember that by getting cross you do neither yourself nor your horse any good, and will only

Catherston Dazzler when he was third in the Grand Prix Special at Copenhagen in 1994

create more tension for the future. If you find that your horse is really boiling over in the test, then some obedience work afterwards through transitions within all the paces should help make him realise that his previous behaviour was not acceptable. When he is obedient, walk him on a long rein and allow him to relax before taking him back to your vehicle.

However well or badly your horse went during the test, at the salute you should pat him and walk from the arena at A on a long rein.

The Showjumping Round

On entering the ring, canter your horse round the arena to familiarise him with the atmosphere. You are not allowed actually to show him the jumps, but going round fairly

close to them can help a young horse. Wait for the bell, hooter or horn. Your horse should be in a forward balanced canter and you should go through the start flags and ride positively towards the first fence, always allowing the fences to come to you, and thinking ahead to the next. Make full use of the corners, using the whole ring, keeping the impulsion, and preparing and getting your horse straight for each fence. You should ride with rhythm and balance, and try to avoid rushing or pulling at your horse which is usually a result of your lack of forward thinking or planning.

When you have jumped the last fence and gone through the finish, don't forget to reward your horse with a pat on the neck, and then leave the arena as soon as possible.

He might appreciate a mouthful of grass to show him he has done well, and put a rug over him. If you went clear you should check with the steward if the jump-off order is to be drawn, or if it is in the first round order. Learn the jump-off course and plan your route carefully, and check how many competitors there are left to go. If the order is drawn you should have your horse warmed up ready in case you are drawn first.

Should the horse go badly or have a fence down, there is no point in getting cross with him, as is so often seen – a horse cannot remember what happened three fences previously, and reprimanding him after you have left the ring or finished your round will make him tense and fearful; this will risk spoiling his whole jumping technique as he will tighten his back in future. It is also an extremely bad example to any young riders who may be watching. If you are eliminated, then you may re-jump the first fence, making sure that it is not being altered by the arena party, or you should leave the ring and jump a practice fence or two before taking your horse back to your vehicle. In this case further schooling at home is necessary, and perhaps a smaller course or a clear round jumping would be a good idea to regain his confidence before you embark again at that level of competition.

The Cross-Country
It is important that you walk the course carefully, taking into account all the alternative routes and making sure you know at each fence where you are approaching from, and in which direction you are going. It will depend on the horse you are riding and his state of training as to whether you take an easier alternative (usually a more circuitous

and therefore time-consuming route) or whether you ride the direct lines with therefore a more forward approach to the fence. If you are uncertain of how a fence is going to ride, it is always a help to see a few horses ridden over it, if this is possible with the times you have been allocated.

Immediately before you are due to start you will be called up by the starter who will warn you how long you have to go; he will then probably warn you at a minute, then at thirty seconds and at ten seconds, when you should go into the starting box and quietly walk round inside the flags. He will count you down from five, and as he says 'go', move your horse from walk to canter and gradually push him up to the rein and into a sensible, balanced speed, especially when riding into the first few fences which you must approach really positively as the young horse will not be fully aware of what is being asked of him. You don't want to rush him round his first event, but confident, forward riding to every fence is important; moreover you must be aware of keeping his concentration, and not let him be distracted by spectators. Keep his adrenalin running, but don't over-excite him. Think of having a good rhythm throughout the course, and when you have landed over the last fence ride smoothly through the finish and pull him up slowly in a straight line,

WARMING UP
When warming up for showjumping, don't sit on your horse in a daze waiting for your turn then suddenly expect him to go in and jump. Keep him on his toes, up to the bridle and mentally alert; if he is the fizzy type walk him quietly, sitting calmly yourself, and enter the ring confidently and in balance.

balancing him between your leg and rein until he is in walk. Do *not* land on his neck, giving him hugs and kisses, totally puffed out yourself, and then sit on top of him to walk back to the vehicle. He might be tired and out of breath, too – though neither of you should be if you were fit enough! – so help him by keeping both him and yourself in balance, and getting off him when you have pulled up.

Loosen his girth and noseband, and keep him walking until he has stopped blowing or you have got back to your vehicle, when you can take off his tack, boots or bandages and wash him off if he has sweated up and needs refreshing. Put on a sweat rug, and a cooler or day rug depending on the weather and wind, and continue walking until he has stopped blowing completely. Check his legs for cuts, grazes or bangs that he may have acquired during the course, and if any are found, wash them off and treat them accordingly. At this stage you can give him a drink if he would like one, though limit it to about half a bucket – two gallons – to start with. If the weather permits he can be led around for some grass, to let him know that he has been good, or alternatively he can be bandaged up for travelling, loaded into the vehicle and given a small feed and/or a haynet.

It is quite common for horses to get upset and difficult in the starting box, especially if they are the excitable sort and enjoy the cross-country phase. I have also had a few which were difficult to get into the starting box, though they quietened down if you were relaxed and quiet and gently kept them moving. We would lead a horse like this into the box either on the countdown of the last five seconds, or would even wait until the starter

Catherston Dazzler with Lizzie in 1991, when he was fourth at Tweseldown and second at Borough Court. This broad education tested the horse's courage and gave him a sensible outlook on life before he specialised in dressage

Western Morn at Badminton in 1973, with Jane Holderness-Roddam. He appears to be enjoying the bigger fences here, and he loved the galloping courses, but he was very awkward and wasted time when his rider tried to collect him for the more trappy combinations

had said 'go' before quietly leading him into the box and gently letting go; he would then be asked to trot out of the box, slowly progressing to canter.

Another horse I had went beautifully over about ten fences on one particular course, and then stopped in the middle of the field and would go no further! Gentle persuading had no effect; a sharp smack made her stand on her hind legs; in fact I couldn't even walk her back to the lorry mounted: the only way I could make her move was to get off her and lead her back to the lorry. I arranged with the secretary to take this horse schooling round

the course later in the day when everything was finished, and exactly the same thing happened. This time, however, I stayed on her and waited: every time she tried to stand on her hind legs she got turned in several small circles on both reins until she was fairly giddy. After approximately twenty minutes she decided to move forwards again, and went on to jump the rest of the course. I came back again to the same place where she had stopped and she did drop the bit, but only for a moment; I made her go on and jump a few more fences before pulling her up and rewarding her.

This mare went on to win

Windsor one-day event, and was placed in several other events in the early 1970s; she was subsequently sold to a friend for his daughter to event. She got on very well with the mare and hunted her over the winter, but then at her first horse trial disaster struck when the mare did exactly the same with this young girl. I went and rode the horse at an event in their area and she tried to do the same thing with me, but then soon took up the bit again and finished the course well. However, we decided that she was a one-rider horse, so took her back and replaced her with a gelding which proved very successful. The mare had further training on the flat, and although she was a beautiful jumper and appeared to enjoy it, we did not feel it was fair to destine her for horse trials; we therefore sold her to Germany as a dressage horse where she became a top class Prix St Georges horse, and subsequently trained many young riders at this level. The extraordinary thing was that the dam of this mare had behaved in exactly the same manner at the very same event! Is this hereditary?

PLANNING THE YOUNG HORSE'S CAREER

Having completed your first competition you now need to plan the course of action you are going to take with your young horse. If all went well, then you will probably have quite a good idea of which competitions you could go to in your area to continue his education. You must take note of the conditions and the going that you will encounter, and consider what is best for your horse at his stage of training; remember that as a five-year-old he will be better able to

COPING WITH ELIMINATION
If your cross-country round did not go according to plan and you were eliminated, then you should leave the course at a walk by the most direct route, keeping out of the way of the other competitors. It would be sensible to go to the secretary of the horse trials to see if the course was going to be available for cross-country schooling the next day; you might be able to overcome your difficulties with the aid of a lead, and more time for your horse to look and learn about the problem concerned.

cope with varying conditions.

If your first competition did not go as well as you hoped, then now is the time to go back to the drawing board and work out what went wrong and why, and what action you need to take in your schooling programme to overcome the difficulties encountered. Don't be in a hurry to take your young horse out again, as one bad competition followed by another will do neither you nor him any good at all.

A novice dressage horse can compete in probably one or two tests a day for the first few competitions, and probably anything between two and three competitions every fortnight would be a maximum for a four-year-old; and if the ground became hard and slippery I would give him a break, with no competitions at all. Potential Dressage Horse classes are ideal for the young horse: these are judged more like a showing class, and this gives the young dressage horse a change from always doing a test in an arena.

We did this with Catherston Humbug; on his first outing it was very windy, and he was also rather excited at being away from home, so I took him away from the horseboxes and lunged him with some fairly short side-reins until he

Dutch Gold has had a long and varied career, and is an excellent example of how a horse can do well in more than one discipline

Dutch Gold as a 3-year-old colt, just broken in, his entire future ahead of him. His rider was planning a career in dressage for him, but he experienced other disciplines first

Dutch Gold winning the Midland Bank Championships at Locko Park in 1983. A good dressage, a clear showjumping round and a steady cross-country on very hard ground brought success for Don Bannocks, his owner at the time. The next day the horse was on a boat to Rotterdam, where he competed in his first international dressage competitions at Prix St George and Intermediare level, with good placings

Warming up for international dressage at Goodwood

Dutch Gold in long-reins aged 18, giving a demonstration of all the Grand Prix movements without the rider

Catherston Dance in the Dark, with Corinne up, jumping at his first show with great confidence and bringing back money on his card

had settled down and I thought him safe to mount, after at least fifteen minutes of showing off! When I mounted him I kept him away from the other horses to start with, as I was really not sure how this young entire would settle; but he behaved, and was introduced to the other horses before he went into the ring for his class. He was fourth, and this outing brought him on a lot both mentally and physically, so that on his second outing he behaved impeccably, without being lunged, and was placed second in a very strong class, thereby qualifying for the finals. He also did his first preliminary dressage test at this show, which he won convincingly by twenty points. I was particularly pleased with the way he managed to balance himself, as the going was quite muddy and the arena fairly

deep, especially for a big horse, but his training had obviously prepared him well so he was able to cope. Because this horse is busy with his stud duties he will not go out many times until the end of the stud season; he will then compete in the Potential Competition Horse classes for eventers, showjumpers and dressage horses. It will be interesting to see how he is judged under saddle, having won it in hand as a three-year-old!

After a successful first event, the event horse can look towards one-day events, as well as dressage and showjumping competitions, although with a good five-year-old you must be careful not to get carried away and do too much, too soon. A good horse takes everything in his stride, but he should really only do Pre-Novice events to start with, and perhaps a couple of Novices when he has enough experience. One event every fortnight at the maximum should be enough for him, and this should preferably be interspersed with the occasional pure dressage competition and some showjumping shows. Riding the BHS Dressage Group tests, or the American Horse Shows Association (AHSA) dressage tests, instead of the Horse Trials tests is a good way of keeping the horse sweet and giving him a change, as horses can be very quick to learn where they go in a test and what they do. There is nothing worse than sitting on a horse in free walk on a long rein when he knows that there is a canter transition coming up in the corner and jogs in anticipation. Overcome this by practising your free walk on a long rein, collecting your horse in walk, and then *walking* a small circle where you would normally canter; continue in walk and trot somewhere else.

The showjumping horse can

Catherston Dazzler at 5 years old, a Potential Competition Horse champion and winner of Horse and Hound's *showjumping prize*

Dance in the Dark with Corinne Bracken, jumping with great style and confidence at his first show at Catherston Stud

compete probably once every week, and at a show he may well be able to do two classes after his first few shows. It does the jumper no harm to do the odd dressage test – contrary to popular belief – as the basics of dressage are the foundation of the showjumper's training: he needs to be supple, obedient, responsive and well balanced so he can cope with jumping a round, and a responsive, balanced horse will be better able to cope with the jump-off. A jumper must be able to increase and decrease his stride immediately he is asked, and to maintain the balance and outline required to clear a fence, and this can only be achieved by building up his muscles correctly, and improving his agility and suppleness so he can change speed and direction easily.

It depends on the age of your horse as to what you can or should do with him: I personally feel that a four-year-old should not do more than dressage and the occasional showjumping class, with perhaps some early cross-country training in the autumn when the ground is softer and the horse a little more mature in his physique. I don't like a four-year-old to compete regularly in jumping classes as I feel this can damage his joints, which are not fully mature until he is five. A competition now and again will bring on a four-year-old horse quite quickly, giving him a little experience which he can absorb into his mind; as a five-year-old he will then be more settled in his attitude when he starts his career for real. An event horse cannot compete in BHS horse trials until he is five (in the US a horse can compete in AHSA horse trials at Novice and training levels as a four-year-old, but must be five for Preliminary level or above), but the occasional hunter trial as a mature four-year-old in the autumn,

on good going, is to be recommended; he will then have time to digest his new lessons over the winter before starting his eventing career in the spring.

As youngsters, both Catherston Dance in the Dark and Catherston Jetstream had some schooling sessions at home with their jumping rider before they went to their first

CATHERSTON STUD

outdoor summer competition together. This was to a local affiliated show where they both jumped clears and were included in the minor placings; this was very exciting for us, and we were delighted with the way they both went. Jetstream was at first quite amazed by the different coloured fences as she had never seen a purple and pink filler before, or a viaduct wall, so was rather spooky and jerky in the first round. Then in the second round she had obviously decided she knew all these colours now and there was no problem whatsoever! Dance in the Dark was his usual 'cool dude' self and took the whole situation in his stride, with the occasional bounce and the odd serpentine in between fences, so that in the second round he was ridden more forwards to make him pay attention and to stop him fooling around.

Both horses went back the next day (it was a two-day show) and confirmed how much they had learnt the day before: both improved

on their performances and came home with their first bit of money on their record cards. The following weekend they went off to a 'proper' three-day showjumping show which had all the big classes as well as the novice ones! They were stabled on the showground and jumped in two classes each day, except Jetstream

Jetstream with Corinne, also at her first jumping show at Langford Farm, where she was placed. She, too, has exceptionally good style

who only did one on the last day as she was tired, both mentally and physically. This show brought both horses on tremendously.

On this occasion the importance of riding a horse in tack which suits him was clearly brought home to us: Dance in the Dark wasn't coping with the changes of direction and

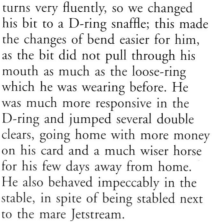

turns very fluently, so we changed his bit to a D-ring snaffle; this made the changes of bend easier for him, as the bit did not pull through his mouth as much as the loose-ring which he was wearing before. He was much more responsive in the D-ring and jumped several double clears, going home with more money on his card and a much wiser horse for his few days away from home. He also behaved impeccably in the stable, in spite of being stabled next to the mare Jetstream.

Jetstream was fairly worried at being away from home and did not eat too well for the first twenty-four hours, but then she got hungry and realised that it wasn't as bad as she first thought! She jumped extremely well, and is now taking on courses with much more confidence; she has matured from the experience tremendously, and is now happy jumping at a higher level. Both of these horses will be taking on the bigger classes later in the season, in the hope that they will qualify for next year's showjumping finals.

YOUR COMPETITION HORSE AND THE FUTURE

Having trained your horse to this level you should now be able to plan his future for the years to come: his early training will have revealed and developed his natural talents so you can determine the discipline to which he is most suited. Try to give yourself and your horse an aim and a goal; after all, you don't know how far you can go as a rider when you have a very good horse under you, until you try! You could both become stars, and have the greatest fun in the world, as long as you trust each other and have that understanding and rapport which makes any partnership successful.

The Catherston Horses Featured

CATHERSTON DANCE IN THE DARK

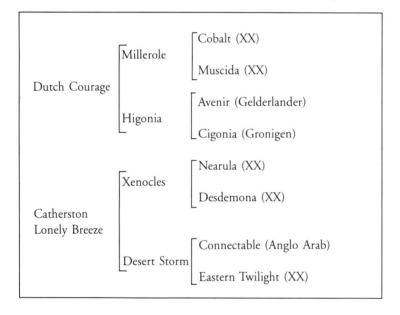

Dutch Courage
- Millerole
  - Cobalt (XX)
  - Muscida (XX)
- Higonia
  - Avenir (Gelderlander)
  - Cigonia (Gronigen)

Catherston Lonely Breeze
- Xenocles
  - Nearula (XX)
  - Desdemona (XX)
- Desert Storm
  - Connectable (Anglo Arab)
  - Eastern Twilight (XX)

Bay stallion, 16hh, born in 1989
Dance in the Dark was a late four-year-old to early five-year-old when this book was written. He is a graded stallion, and by the time he was competing as described in this book he had already had two crops of foals. The plans for his immediate future are to send him showjumping and eventing in the autumn, as a late five-year-old, to establish which discipline he is most suited to. We are leaving him until the autumn because he is quite busy in the spring time with his stud duties.

CATHERSTON HUMBUG

```
Liboi ─────────┬─── Tom Rolfe ──────┬─── Ribot (XX)
               │                    │
               │                    └─── Pocahontas (XX)
               │
               └─── Latin Walk ─────┬─── Roman Tread (XX)
                                    │
                                    └─── Stall Walker (XX)

Catherston ────┬─── Dutch ──────────┬─── Millerole (XX)
Doodlebug      │    Courage         │
               │                    └─── Higonia (Gron / Geld)
               │
               └─── Cedola ─────────┬─── Commandeur (Gron)
                                    │
                                    └─── Bedola (Gron)
```

Brown stallion, 16.2hh, born in 1990

Humbug was a late three-year-old to an early four-year-old when this book was written. His career plans destine him to be a dressage horse, though he may also do some jumping and eventing to broaden his capabilities and prove himself as a graded stallion. His first foals look outstanding.

CATHERSTON ZEBEDEE

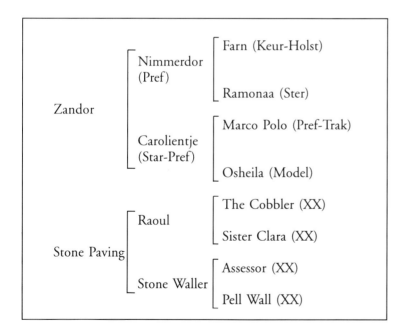

```
Zandor ────────┬─── Nimmerdor ──────┬─── Farn (Keur-Holst)
               │    (Pref)          │
               │                    └─── Ramonaa (Ster)
               │
               └─── Carolientje ────┬─── Marco Polo (Pref-Trak)
                    (Star-Pref)     │
                                    └─── Osheila (Model)

Stone Paving ──┬─── Raoul ──────────┬─── The Cobbler (XX)
               │                    │
               │                    └─── Sister Clara (XX)
               │
               └─── Stone Waller ───┬─── Assessor (XX)
                                    │
                                    └─── Pell Wall (XX)
```

Bay stallion, 16.1hh, born in 1990

Zebedee was a late three-year-old to a rising four-year-old when this book was written. He is a graded stallion and has had one crop of foals. Zebedee is aimed for the showjumping career that his breeding suggests. We have kept him quiet as a four-year-old, waiting until he is fully grown and matured before pressing on with his jumping career as a five-year-old. He appears to be a horse with a great future and a mountain of potential, but we have to curb our enthusiasm and not ask too much of him too soon.

CATHERSTON JETSTREAM

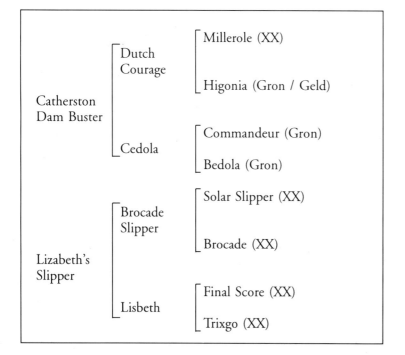

```
                    ┌ Aldis Lamp
         ┌ Le Farquin
         │          └ Fagne
 Jashin ─┤
         │          ┌ Wiardus
         └ Era ─────┤
                    └ unknown

                              ┌ Millerole (XX)
                    ┌ Dutch ──┤
                    │ Courage └ Higonia (Gron / Geld)
 Catherston ────────┤
 Dutch Sika         │          ┌ Welton Gameful (XX)
                    └ Welton ──┤
                      Gazelle  └ Lisa
```

Chestnut mare, 16.2hh, born in 1988

This mare was broken and ridden for two months before being put in foal at four years old; she produced a lovely bay colt by Liboi (XX). This colt is called Catherston Liberator. Jetstream came back into work as a six-year-old, when she started her career as a jumper. The pictures of her in this book were when she was rising six. Her career plans are that she will be a showjumper, and then later a brood mare.

CATHERSTON DEAR EDWARD

```
                              ┌ Millerole (XX)
                    ┌ Dutch ──┤
                    │ Courage └ Higonia (Gron / Geld)
 Catherston ────────┤
 Dam Buster         │          ┌ Commandeur (Gron)
                    └ Cedola ──┤
                               └ Bedola (Gron)

                              ┌ Solar Slipper (XX)
                    ┌ Brocade ─┤
                    │ Slipper  └ Brocade (XX)
 Lizabeth's ────────┤
 Slipper            │          ┌ Final Score (XX)
                    └ Lisbeth ─┤
                               └ Trixgo (XX)
```

Chestnut gelding, 16.2hh, born in 1990

At the time of writing this book Edward was a late three-year-old to early four-year-old. He competed successfully in preliminary and affiliated novice dressage as a four-year-old, and was subsequently sold to America as a young dressage horse.

Index

Page numbers in *italics* indicate illustrations